Encyclopedia of

Garden
Design
& Structure

ENCYCLOPEDIA *of* Garden Design & Structure

IDEAS AND INSPIRATION FOR YOUR GARDEN

Derek Fell

D&C
David and Charles

Page 1: A wrought iron gate and dry wall make a bold contrast of metal and stone.
Page 2: A beautiful vista viewed from a deck, showing three changes of elevation, each defined by different design elements. First, a meandering brick path, then a flight of rough fieldstone steps, and finally a sunlit lawn framed by trees.
Page 4: Wildlife pond reflection doubles the beauty of its surroundings in a woodland garden that features a summerhouse for taking tea.
Page 5 (from top): Arched Japanese bridge painted red contrasts boldly with a predominantly green background. Arbor of espaliered apple trees, Eleutherian Mills garden, USA. Teak bench on brick paving, surrounding a millstone.

A DAVID & CHARLES BOOK

David & Charles is an F+W Publications Inc. company
4700 East Galbraith Road
Cincinnati, OH 45236

First published in the UK by David & Charles Ltd. in 2005
First published in New Zealand by David Bateman Ltd.
in 2005

Copyright © Derek Fell & David Bateman Ltd. 2005

Derek Fell has asserted his right to be identified as author of this work in accordance with the Copyright, Designs and Patents Act, 1988.

A catalogue record for this book is available from the British Library.

ISBN 0 7153 2227 3 Hardback
ISBN 0 7153 2228 1 Paperback

Printed in China through Colorcraft Ltd.
for David & Charles
Brunel House   Newton Abbot   Devon

Visit our website at www.davidandcharles.co.uk

David & Charles books are available from all good bookshops; alternatively you can contact our Orderline on 0870 9908222 or write to us at FREEPOST EX2110, David & Charles Direct, Newton Abbot, TQ12 4ZZ (no stamp required UK mainland).

Contents

Introduction

Designing the landscape

Garden writers, landscape architects and garden historians frequently debate what it is that makes a garden great and inspirational. Though opinions are diverse, many experts agree that a great garden must display a sense of artistry, using the sky and soil as a canvas and plants and structures as 'paint' to create a visually exciting space that can be formal or informal in style, large or small in size. Moreover, great gardens can exist in a wide range of settings, from the highly artificial environment of a city to stimulating natural surroundings such as that of a Scottish loch, a Normandy river valley or a Carolina coastal swamp.

When painters seek artistic development and inspiration they visit great art collections, like those in the Louvre, Paris, the Tate Gallery, London, and the Getty Museum, Los Angeles. When gardeners seek inspiration there is no one place to find a wide selection of styles and designs, hence the reason for this book. Though it may reflect a personal appreciation of garden designs, it is a convenient collection of stimulating garden features from all over the world, aimed at presenting a gallery of useful ideas in an encyclopedic listing for ready reference.

Gardens of inspiration

The great French Impressionist painter, Claude Monet, considered his garden at Giverny, north of Paris, his greatest work of art, and as many as a hundred special design ideas can be gleaned from visiting the restored garden today. In his Clos Normand flower garden, these include visually exciting color harmonies such as his hot-color borders, using mostly yellow, orange and red flowers. Another Monet innovation is the floral tunnel, his Grande Allée. He used climbing roses on arches to create the roof and perennials, such as asters, to form the sides. Nasturtiums planted to creep across the path completed the tunnel effect.

In Monet's water garden, a Japanese-style arched bridge with a canopy of blue and white wisteria is probably the most familiar garden structure ever made, and the inspiration for many bridges like it worldwide.

Since artistry is so important to a garden's success, many of the design ideas for this book are from the restored gardens of Monet and his painter friends, Renoir and Cezanne. Other images have been selected from inspirational gardens all over the world, not only public gardens in Europe, the Americas,

Opposite *Cezanne's garden, Aix-en-Provence.* **Above** *Monet's garden, Giverny.* **Above right** *Renoir's frost-free garden, near Nice.* **Right** *Cedaridge Farm, Pennsylvania.*

Africa and Australasia, but also little-known private gardens.

A study of Paul Cezanne's half-acre restored garden at Aix-en-Provence, and Auguste Renoir's five-acre restored garden near Nice reveals startling design innovation quite different from that of Monet. Though all three artists were friends and identified with the Impressionist movement, their gardens are as different as their painting styles. While Monet created a labor-intensive design using mostly flowers to 'paint' his outdoors sanctuary, and taking color high on trellises and arches, Cezanne planted a labor-saving garden using less ephemeral elements of nature. His restored garden is essentially a shade garden, terraced with quarry stones and filled with trees and shrubs that paint a tapestry of foliage colors, their trunks pruned to create eerie sinuous lines.

Renoir purchased an old olive orchard to save it from development and created a retreat where he could pose nudes as though they were sitting in shadowy woodland on the upper slope of his property. He also seated models on a sun-drenched wildflower meadow at the lower part. Like Monet, who built a boat so he could paint his water garden from the middle of his pond, Renoir constructed a rustic shelter with floor-to-ceiling windows so he could paint the main tree-lined vista during inclement weather, his nude model seated outside in dappled light.

Even the well-respected Victorian garden designer, Gertrude Jekyll, gleaned ideas for her plantings from studying the work of the great French Impressionist painters.

Many of the ideas featured in this book are from my own garden, historic Cedaridge Farm, in Bucks County, Pennsylvania. They have been realized from studying gardens worldwide, never slavishly copied, but adapted to the environment of an historic farm dating back to 1791, and similar to the historic farm Renoir purchased as his home in Provence. At Cedaridge Farm there are no power lines visible, and like Renoir we try to maintain an old-fashioned appearance, making repairs with rusty hinges and nails, and never minding if shutters show peeling paint. Spring and autumn are cool, summers are hot and humid, and winters invariably bring snow and cold that will freeze the ground solid to the depth of a spade. As a consequence of creating twenty theme areas connected by a stroll path, the garden has received several awards for design excellence, including 'Best Interpretation of an Impressionist Garden'.

Informal versus formal design

The years between 1600 and 1900 saw formal garden design hugely popular, particularly in Europe and North America. In recent years formality has experienced a decline, perhaps because people today see enough formality in their daily lives and yearn for more intimacy with nature. Also, informal gardens generally are less costly than formal ones, which often require expensive stonework and regular pruning of hedges to keep the design sharply defined. Therefore, the first design decision when contemplating the creation of a garden is to determine whether it should be formal or informal, or a combination of the two disciplines.

Popular examples of formal gardens are those created in Italy during the Renaissance, such as the Villa Lante and Villa d'Este, which in turn inspired the great French gardens of Vaux-le-Vicomte and Versailles, and the California garden of Hearst Castle, weekend retreat of newspaper magnate the late Randolph Hearst. Japanese and Chinese gardens, with their emphasis on stone, water and evergreen trees, are also considered formal because the dynamics of both garden styles rely heavily on exaggeration through pruning and mounding, and the precise placement of stone and water features, even though the end result is not as formal as the Italian model.

Informal gardens have always existed around country cottages of Europe, particularly in Normandy and England, but it was the publisher William Robinson, and one of his contributors, Gertrude Jekyll, who rebelled against the formality of Victorian carpet bedding to advocate informal garden designs for estates, inspiring the planting of meadow gardens, rock gardens and woodland gardens, using flowering plants generously and naturalistically.

Softscape versus hardscape components

Though many garden spaces, such as meadow gardens, can be made entirely by using plants ('softscape' to use the term preferred by landscape architects), it is often the use of structural elements (or 'hardscape') which produces the strongest sense of design. These hardscape elements can be highly functional (like bridges and paths) or strictly ornamental (like sculpture and fountains).

It should be realized that the more hardscape used for a garden, the less labor-intensive it is likely to be. Woody plants generally do not need the upkeep of herbaceous plants like annuals and perennials, which explains the liking among many modern designers to create minimalist gardens, where a potted plant with a strong sculptural quality, like a candelabra euphorbia (*Euphorbia candelabrum*), may be the only embellishment to a courtyard.

Seasonal considerations

It is sometimes difficult to keep a garden picture-perfect through all four seasons, and so it may be desirable to go for a big boost of color during a favorite season. Spring is an obvious first choice because it is a welcome respite from winter's bleakness, and more floral color can be concentrated into spring than any other time. Rainfall is usually plentiful, while summer months can bring drought. However, meadow gardens can look their best in mid to late summer, and the same can be true of water gardens, for waterlilies flower more profusely during summer months.

Gardens that rely on trees and shrubs for visual excitement can look sensational in autumn. Although winter is a season of dormancy for many plants, it is a good time to study gardens because essential design elements such as bridges, gazebos, benches, paths and pools can best be appreciated without the distraction of flowering plants and dense foliage cover. Outlined and defined with a dusting of frost or snow, strong design elements can be accentuated.

A definition of terms

When a new garden is contemplated, there are several kinds of professional help that can be considered, and this can lead to confusion. While even large gardens can be accomplished as a do-it-yourself project, with no professional help, many people today will consider employing the services of a landscape architect, a landscape designer (also called a garden designer), and a landscape contractor.

It was Frederick Law Olmsted (the person responsible for landscaping New York City's Central Park) who is credited with coining the term 'landscape architect' to describe a person who professionally performs the function of altering and planting the land. Legally and conceptually there are differences between a landscape architect and a landscape designer (or garden designer).

Landscape architects must take several years of training, and pass a test to be licensed in most countries. On the other hand, a landscape designer, or garden designer, can have no formal training, and can be anyone who designs outdoor spaces, using primarily plants and rudimentary hardscape elements, such as decks and patios. Though both a landscape architect and a landscape designer may be capable of producing a site plan, it is the landscape contractor who takes the approved drawings and uses construction equipment like bulldozers and backhoes to move earth and lay stone.

Top *The Golden Pavilion garden, Kyoto, Japan.* **Above** *Court of the Pool, Alhambra and Generalife gardens, Granada.*

Early inspiration

A lot of great garden design is learned from the distant past. Some of the first gardens of which we have knowledge were created in Persia, by sultans, about 3000 BC. Denoting wealth and power, these highly formal spaces were walled to keep out drifting sand, and laid out in a geometric quadrant design, with rills dividing the outer square into smaller squares. A basin or water fountain usually marked the middle, and water channels tapping run-off from distant snow-covered mountains were designed to irrigate fruit trees such as almonds and figs through underground conduits that sometimes extended thirty miles. Invariably, one end of the garden would feature a raised pavilion, richly draped with curtains, as a place for entertaining and feasting and taking in the garden view.

About 1500 BC, emperors in China began to establish gardens as a symbol of prestige, and we know that the Emperor Wu, at the height of the Roman Empire in Europe, was inspired to create a garden out of a religious belief that immortals dwelled in a land known as the Mystic Isles. Failing to find the Mystic Isles within his domain, he constructed a lake with islands to represent the Mystic Isles of his imagination, and the shorelines were landscaped to represent a rocky coast. Later, with the advent of Buddhism, Chinese monks developed similar lake-and-island gardens as part of their monastic life, and also as a reminder that the souls of believers of Buddhism dwelt in a blissful landscape surrounded by the fragrance of flowers and the sounds of celestial music. These visually soothing places were rich in symbolism to show veneration of nature, using manmade mounds to represent hills, boulders brought down from mountains to represent rocky islands, and specially pruned conifers to recreate the reverence and serenity of trees twisted and shaped by adversity. These early Chinese gardens greatly influenced Japanese gardens, which became more highly refined as uplifting, spiritual places.

The Garden of Eden, referred to in the Bible as the home of Adam and Eve, was a sanctuary where 'everything that is pleasant to the sight and good for food' grew without effort. A common concept of paradise, the Garden of Eden is portrayed in most religious and botanical art as a woodland-and-water garden, containing a rich collection of exotic plants, like a botanical garden. With the decline of Rome and the spread of Christianity, gardens throughout Europe were cloistered inside monasteries as a means of being self-sufficient. These contained mostly edible and medicinal plants, often in raised beds using boards on edge or low woven wicker fences to contain the soil. They were laid out in squares dissected by paths, often with a well at the center as a functional focal point, or a stone crucifix as a symbol of Biblical inspiration.

The Arab prophet, Mohammed, was born in Mecca about AD570. Inspired by the Old Testament, he founded the religion known as Islam, independent of Christianity. By the 8th century, Islam extended from Morocco in the west to India in the east. In his book of the Koran, Mohammed predicted that a Day of Judgement would decide who could enter a beauti-

ful pleasure garden and live in perpetual tranquility, shaded by trees and cooled by spring-fed streams. In later centuries wealthy followers of Mohammed created their own pleasure gardens as havens of tranquility on earth.

Today, the best surviving examples of Islamic gardens are at the Alhambra Palace, in Granada, dating to the 1400s when the Moors (Islamic Moroccans) occupied Spain. These are mostly courtyards laid out in a formal grid design of multiple quadrants, like the early Persian gardens, but with even more embellishment, using colorful tile work to edge water channels, and an enclosure of arched passages featuring intricate stone fretwork to resemble lace.

Soon after the expulsion of the Moors from Spain, cardinals of the Vatican, in Italy, as symbols of their prestige and power began to create incredibly ornate gardens, the most ostentatious of which is the Villa d'Este, near Rome. Constructed on a steep hillside, it is a terraced garden with a long main central axis of steps. The wide terraces feature immense water cascades and fountains, baroque statuary and water channels. The Villa d'Este inspired the great French formal garden of Vaux-le-Vicomte, home of Louis XIV's finance minister, Nicolas Fouquet. Lacking a steep hillside to build upon, Fouquet's designer, André Le Nôtre, laid out his main axis and water features on flat ground southeast of Paris. The garden's completion was marked by a fantastic

fireworks display. Feeling belittled by the magnificence of Vaux-le-Vicomte, the Sun King had its owner imprisoned, and instructed Fouquet's designer to overshadow Vaux with a new palace, Versailles, northwest of Paris.

Many of the gardens of British aristocracy, such as Hampton Court Palace, Stourhead and Chatsworth, were inspired by Versailles and a desire to show prestige and status.

In America, Gooch and Spottiswood, early governors of Colonial Williamsburg, Virginia, brought order to the visual chaos of a forest wilderness by creating a splendid formal garden around the Governor's Palace. A canal was built for ladies and gentlemen to stroll around, geometric patterns of boxwood were installed, and pleached alleys of hornbeam were established, along with a beautiful, neat-as-a-pin, walled kitchen garden. The royal governors were proud of their miniature Versailles, but the local population saw it as an extravagant waste of their taxes, fueling the first stirrings of unrest which turned into the conflagration of the American Revolution.

Expressing one's individuality

When a focus group of baby boomers was recently asked what they most wanted in a garden, the result was surprising. Not only did the majority of respondents want a garden that expressed their own individuality, they preferred to have another person – a professional – design and plant that garden for them.

How does one express individuality in a garden? First, by deciding its primary purpose. For example, should it be a quiet, secluded sanctuary screened from a busy road and neighbors as a place to unwind; will it be used primarily for outdoor entertaining; or should it be a source of flowers for indoor arrangements? Should it be a minimalist garden for a busy career person, or perhaps a wildlife garden of mostly indigenous plants for a conservationist? Does the garden need to consider children and have a play area and a lawn for games? Must it take into consideration boisterous dogs? Is a water feature important? How much time can an owner spend on essential maintenance? Can the owner afford a landscape service for timely maintenance such as planting, pruning, mulching, fertilizing, soil conditioning, deadheading, irrigation, weeding, and winter clean-up? Should the theme of the garden reflect the owner's personality? For example, a Japanese garden for a collector of Oriental antiques; an Italian garden for someone of Italian heritage; an English cottage garden for an Anglophile; a combination herb-and-vegetable garden for a gourmand? Should all parts be wheelchair-accessible for an invalid in the family?

The well-publicized British coastal garden of the late Derek Jarmans, a set designer for the London theater, expressed his sensitive, earth-friendly, creative personality with a spartan cottage along a pebble shoreline on the Thames estuary, where he brought into the garden items of flotsam and jetsam, like driftwood pitted by barnacles, torn fishing nets and storm ravaged buoys, as sculpture. These he seeded around with indigenous wildflowers like corn poppies and mallow, sea oats and sea kale. All this was developed within view of a hideous nuclear power plant, the very antithesis of Jarman's psychological yearnings.

The garden known as Little Sparta, Scotland, reflects the tenacious, controversial and artistic temperament of its owner, Ian Hamilton Finlay, whose Scottish brogue, when aroused, can make the windows rattle. 'I started to use text in the garden in different kinds of inscription,' he muses, 'It was quite unusual to have inscriptions in classical gardens, and I liked the idea.' He credits misapprehensions with the local council with his inventiveness, for when they pronounced his construction of a garden temple dedicated to the Greek god, Apollo, an art gallery rather than a religious building, in order to collect a tax, it raised his hackles, and made him more obstinate and ideological.

Little Sparta is now filled with replicas of Roman roads and story stones. These story stones include massive broken stone tablets laid beside a pond, as though shattered by earthquake, also a slate memorial to a ship lost at sea and set into a moss-covered stone wall.

There have been many other trend-setting and highly individualistic garden designers like Jarmans and Finlay. Most have written books or had books written about their work. This documentation is not a recent tradition. Pliny the Younger, a first-century Roman statesman, left descriptions

Opposite *Main vista, Vaux-le-Vicomte, France.* **Above** *The parterre garden, Governor's Palace, Williamsburg, Virginia.*

of his gardens at several villas he owned. His surviving plan of Tuscum (near Rome) shows a strong central, sloping axis with views to the Apennine Mountains, and a third of the garden space strictly formal, including life-size topiary animals pruned out of boxwood.

In the 18th century the names of Lancelot 'Capability' Brown (1716–83) and Sir Humphrey Repton (1752–1818) are synonymous with dignified English landscape design. Brown banished regimented formal gardens from around the house in favor of uncluttered vistas across contoured parkland salted with sheep, glittering free-form lakes and clusters of trees. Repton produced beautiful 'before' and 'after' renderings for his clients, showing his romantic concepts which allowed terraces and flowerbeds close to the house again.

Twentieth-century trendsetters

Gertrude Jekyll (1843–1932) worked in collaboration with English architect Sir Edwin Lutyens. She developed beautiful gardens around her home, Munstead Wood, in Surrey, and committed her ideas to print in a series of books, including *Colour Schemes for the Flower Garden* (1914). In private ownership, the gardens at Munstead Wood, noted for its

wide, long, mixed perennial borders, have been restored and are occasionally opened to the public.

Vita Sackville-West (1892–1962) wrote a garden column for the British *Observer* newspaper and authored seven garden books. With her husband, Harold Nicolson, a career diplomat, she created the spectacular 'compartment' garden of Sissinghurst, which is now owned by the National Trust.

Thomas Church (1902–78), the leading landscape architect in California, produced a book about his work entitled *Gardens are for People* (1955) in which he explained his philosophy of designing gardens as outdoor rooms, with an emphasis on places for relaxation. Church's counterpart in Europe was Russell Page (1906–85) who wrote *The Education of a Gardener* (1962), documenting gardens he designed in France, Italy, Belgium, Switzerland and the USA, with an eye for formality and easy maintenance.

Roberto Burle Marx (1909–1994) was a leading landscape architect in Brazil who greatly influenced tropical gardens worldwide. His style is instantly recognizable for contrasting strong modernistic architectural elements, such as Inca-inspired walls and canal-like watercourses, with dense plantings of tropical species in huge swathes. Other signatures include the use of giant forms of philodendron vines, eye-catching bromeliads in bold terracotta containers, and huge Victoria waterlily 'platters'. His garden near Rio was deeded to the state on his death, and is open to the public.

Living trendsetters are harder to identify. The naturalistic plantings of Dutchman Piet Oudolf have become extremely popular in Europe, weaving ornamental grasses and plants with wispy, see-through blossoms among drifts of flowering perennials to create an artistic, free-flowing tapestry, a style also popularized by Dutch artist Ton ter Linden. In the US the design team of Ohme and van Sweden have made this style of gardening significant over much of their careers. Mien Ruys, Penelope Hobhouse and Beth Chatto have also taken garden design in new directions.

For distinctive structural elements look to the work of Andy Goldsworthy, who fashions stones and branches into organic sculptural forms such as stone cairns and woven twig structures. Many of his designs feature a black circular hole. Though the symbolism of the black hole seems sexual, he describes it as a dimension that completes a whole, black signifying the heart of a stone or the heart of a tree, like a cave or hollow with something tantalizing and mysterious inside. His own garden, Glenluce, in Dumfrieshire, Scotland, utilizes centuries-old buildings and walls of a farm as backgrounds for his sculpture. 'If I had to describe my work in one word, that word would be "time",' he says.

Though many of Goldsworthy's creations are fleeting, using wildflower petals and ice formations, some are durable, such as the 2278 ft long, snaking Storm King Wall at the Storm King Art Center, New York State. Inspired by British farm walls common in Wales and the Yorkshire dales, it has no mortar for support. In an age when art in the garden has become abstract and contrived, it is comforting to see how Goldsworthy produces unconventional patterns and sculptures with whatever he discovers in the outdoors – branches, foliage, rocks, ice formations, flower petals and even pigeon feathers – to provoke new ways to look at the wonders of nature and the magic of the garden.

Opposite *Roberto Burle Marx landscape, Brazil.* **Left** *Border of see-through perennials by Ton ter Linden, Holland.*
Bottom *Goldsworthy's Storm King Wall, New York State.*

Garden design and structure

An encyclopedic listing

In the following encyclopedic listing of information and ideas, space prohibits the inclusion of every type of design feature that can be employed in the making of a beautiful garden. The list has been confined to 120 categories deemed to be most important for contemporary tastes. They represent ideas for both formal and informal design concepts, in all seasons, many climates, including tropical and sub-tropical, and various topographical locations, including coastal and hillside. Though the pictures show mostly small-space ideas, some expansive designs are included to show the ultimate potential for a concept and because bigness can still be inspirational when designing small spaces.

A balance has been struck between 'softscape' (plantings) and 'hardscape' (structures), and in deciding space for each category, its relative importance in today's design dynamic was considered. This explains the space devoted to both 'Color Theme Gardens', a relatively new design consideration, and 'Paths', which were among the first design features conceived for a pleasure garden.

Definitions sometimes create confusion. The term 'gazebo' – strictly speaking a decorative shelter from which to admire a view – can be called a belvedere, kiosk, temple, teahouse, pagoda, summerhouse, pavilion, and folly, depending on size and design. In the following listing some of these definitions have been separated out; others included under the 'Gazebo' category. They can all serve as architectural beacons in the landscape and a place from which to admire a view, but today they do not necessarily all include a view, since these structures have become popular retreats for reading or quiet contemplation, often in the most secluded part of the garden.

Conservatory with begonias, hydrangeas and impatiens, Royal Tasmanian Botanic Garden, Hobart, Australia.

Alleys and avenues

ALLEYS AND AVENUES are interchangeable words to describe a corridor of trees or shrubs, usually designed to create parallel lines along the entrance driveway to a house. Trees can be encouraged to grow tall by pruning away lower limbs, allowing the topmost branches to arch out and mingle with branches from the opposite line of trees. This then creates a 'cathedral' effect, the trunks and arching branches resembling the vaulted columns of a church or cathedral. In the best examples, the avenue helps to frame an imposing residence, or alternatively a prominent natural or manmade accent, such as a statue, temple, or lake.

The French *allée* is generally a tree- or hedge-bordered walk forming a straight line as part of a formal geometric layout. The *allée* reached its most ostentatious in the gardens of Versailles Palace where the corridors of mostly elms and oaks are up to half a mile long, intersecting to create a criss-crossed grid. Other corridors fan out from a central point to make a goose-foot (*patte-d'oie*). At Hampton Court Palace, England, more than 400 lime trees, planted in the 17th century, are another outstanding example of a goose-foot design.

1 *Monet's Grande Allée, France. 2 Oak Alley, Louisiana.*
3 *Cherry avenue, Dumbarton Oaks, Washington DC.*
4 *Woodland allée at Versailles, France.*

1

2

4

3

The French, with their liking for rigid formality in garden design, are fond of creating pleached *allées*, whereby the trunks are pruned of lower branches to make pillars, and the top-knot of leaves is rigorously pruned to a box shape so the top and sides of the *allée* are flat, creating an aerial hedge.

Monet's garden features a Grande Allée, using metal arches for climbing roses to create a floral tunnel that connects his house to his water garden. Renoir's garden features an *allée* of ancient olive trees; and Cezanne's garden is filled with paths arched over by the branches of mock orange (*Philadelphus*) and Judas tree (*Cercis siliquastrum*) to create leafy tunnels.

At Cedaridge Farm, a leafy tunnel similar to those in Cezanne's garden is a feature of the woodland garden. Native maples and oaks are pruned high to create an arboreal cathedral of green in spring and summer that changes to gold in autumn, and white after frost and snow coat the branches in winter.

Alleys suitable for small-space gardens can be made from closely spaced evergreens, such as arborvitae and yew. When these are trained to create a tunnel and the trunks exposed, its popular definition is a 'ghost walk'.

1 *Scarlet maple corridor at Grounds for Sculpture, New Jersey.*
2 *Live oak avenue at Magnolia Plantation, South Carolina.*
3 *Chestnut avenue and driveway, France.* 4 *Piccabeen palm avenue, Virginia Robinson garden, California.*

1

2

4

3

Animals and animal shelters

ANIMALS AND ANIMAL SHELTERS can be an integral part of gardens, even if it is only a cat or a dog that enjoys freedom of the space. A calico female cat named Fifi patrols the five-acre garden of Claude Monet, helping to control the rodent population (which can girdle young trees and eat the roots of rose-bushes during winter). Though cats can kill a lot of songbirds, a bell around their necks will give warning. Nesting boxes should be placed out of a cat's reach so birds can breed in comparative safety. To be discouraged are most wild-animal visitors such as deer and rabbits, which can be highly destructive of plants.

Animal shelters can range from a decorative dog kennel to an imposing menagerie, made popular during Victorian times for the keeping of exotic animals. Magnolia Plantation, South Carolina, features a petting zoo as part of its garden attractions, and in their swamp garden they have alligator observation decks.

Farm gardens and country estates are natural places to have farm animals in the landscape. A beautiful sheep shelter exists on Cuttalossa Farm, near New Hope, Pennsylvania. Set beside a stream beneath towering American sycamore trees, and enclosed by a split-rail fence, it makes a picturesque rustic accent backed by a slope of native rhododendron. The stream and the tree canopy help to trap moisture in the atmosphere, promoting luxuriant moss growth on the roof.

Friendly dogs are generally a delight to encounter during a stroll through the garden. A miniature collie, or Shetland sheepdog, might be perfectly at home in a small garden where a rumbustious Great Pyrennean mountain dog could do a lot of damage. A chow chow might be amusing to encounter in an Oriental garden.

1 Thoroughbred horses, Château de Sassy, France. 2 Calico cat, Fifi, on Monet's bench. 3 Sheep shelter, Cuttalossa Farm, Pennsylvania. 4 Shetland sheepdog, Henry garden, Pennsylvania.

1

2

4

3

Annual gardens

ANNUAL GARDENS are a quick fix for the landscape, since many annuals can be planted in bud or early bloom. However, annuals are not to everyone's taste, and the American garden writer, the late Carlton B. Lees, warned his readership; 'The weakness of American gardening is the petunia-bed thinking of many who play a leading role in it'.

Though Gertrude Jekyll advised combining annuals with perennials to create mixed borders, she also kept a number of potted annuals on the sidelines to fill gaps in her displays when the perennials faded from the scene. She deplored the practice of bedding out annuals to make garish, uniform floral carpets. The term 'bedding out' describes the Victorian practice of arranging annuals in brightly-colored patterns, while 'carpet bedding' is the planting of annuals of uniform height in carpet-like designs, using foliage or floral color, or a combination of the two.

There are exceptions to the prohibition of using annuals exclusively. For example, at the historic garden of Leaming's Run, New Jersey, a ribbon of scarlet-red salvia effectively leads the eye along a green lawn to a white Victorian gazebo. At Cedaridge Farm, myriad colors of pansies weave a bright, uniform tapestry in front of a Victorian-style gazebo in spring. When the flowering display weakens at the onset of summer, the pansies are replaced by heat-tolerant annuals. At Cedaridge there is also a grouping of blood-red bedding geraniums in terracotta pots, to contrast with stone steps, as seen in the streets of Provence. The mass of one bright color contrasting boldly with the aged gray stone and vigorous green of the geranium leaves is a favorite among visitors.

With the right choice of varieties, the color impact of annuals can be long lasting and intense. Annuals such as 'Queen Sophia' French marigolds, 'Wave' petunias, 'Dreamland' zinnias and 'Salsa' scarlet sage (*Salvia splendens*) are examples of 'everblooming' annuals that are quick to flower from seed and good for sunny locations. For constant color in shade, there are 'Fortuna' impatiens, 'Thousand Wonders' begonias, 'Duchess' torenia and 'Saber' coleus. Bred for uniformity of height to satisfy parks that still like to emulate Victorian carpet bedding, these annuals can be massed within a parterre design (such as clipped boxwood) as a substitute for colored gravel.

Certain annuals work very well in meadow plantings. Indeed, numerous seed companies offer special 'wildflower mixtures' involving annual poppies, African daisies, cornflower, cosmos, baby's breath, larkspur, mallow, catchfly and other varieties that can flower quickly from seed broadcast directly onto bare soil. The variability of heights is part of the appeal and naturalistic appearance.

A key to profuse blooming with annuals is to 'plant green' i.e. use plants showing no flower, and to pinch out the lead shoot at time of transplanting. The pinching encourages side branching, and the lack of flowers on a transplant is generally a good indication that the plant is not stressed. 'Deadheading', the removal of spent flowers to stop them going to seed, is also essential to prolong the flowering display of most annuals.

1

2

1 *Elaborate carpet bedding design, France.* 2 *Formal garden, Caramoor, New York State, featuring wax begonias.*
3 *Mixed summer border in a Christchurch, New Zealand, park.*
4 *Massed 'Appleblossom' petunias, Filoli garden, California.*
5 *Geranium display, Cedaridge Farm.* 6 *Floral ribbon using scarlet sage, Leaming's Run, New Jersey.* 7 *Field of sunflowers.*
8 *Drifts of sunny annuals, San Lois Obispo, California.*
9 *'Hot' coleus border with birdbath.*

3

4

5

6

7

8

9

Arbors and arches

ARBORS AND ARCHES are often interchangeable terms to describe a structure that allows a space to be shaded by vines, although arches can be unadorned, made from wood, metal or stone, and look decorative without further embellishment. One great benefit of an arbor is to provide shade for pausing or sitting. Both arbors and arches can also act as a soothing transition from one garden space to another, to frame a view and carry colorful flowers or foliage above eye level. Arbors can form passages and tunnels to connect widely spaced parts of a garden, and even buildings, in which case they are generally called a 'pergola'.

Excellent hardy vines for arbors include blue and white wisteria, orange and yellow trumpet creeper (*Campsis*), white silver fleece vine (*Fallopia baldschuanica*) and clematis in mostly shades of blue and red, plus white. Wisteria has the added advantage of providing fragrance. Other fragrant flowering vines to consider include honeysuckle, jasmine and climbing roses. A favorite fragrant thornless old garden rose is 'Zéphirine Drouhin', which covers itself with masses of large, double, deep-pink blooms in spring, pervading the air with an uplifting, fruity aroma. 'American Pillar' is another popular climbing rose ideal for high arbors and arches.

Though one usually encounters arbors with only one variety of vine for the canopy, a partnership of plants can be trained to meet in the middle and mingle their blossoms. For example, the orange-flowered 'Westerland' rose and a violet-blue 'Jackmanii' clematis will entwine their stems and flowers to bloom simultaneously in spring. Honeysuckle is also a good companion plant for climbing roses, effective in such combinations as white climbing 'Iceberg' and *Lonicera x heckrottii* 'Gold Flame', which has gold and rose-pink trumpet-shaped blooms.

Do not narrow your focus to flowering plants only. Virginia creeper (*Parthenocissus quinquefolia*) has decorative, ivy-shaped leaves that turn molten red in autumn. Similarly, foliage of the crimson glory grape vine (*Vitis coignetiae*) turns glowing red in autumn, and though the small black fruits are decorative they are inedible. If edible fruit is desired, plant a regular dessert grape, or the hardy kiwi vine (*Actinidia*). Though a male and a female kiwi are needed to yield a harvest, the fruit is delicious.

Do not neglect the base of arches and arbors. For the shady parts consider hostas, heucheras and ferns. These will help to soften the hard lines of uprights and spill into the path.

Arches make good entrances to theme gardens. The style of arch can introduce the theme. For example, a moon-gate style of arch would be ideal at the entrance to a Chinese garden, and an arch made from whale jawbones appropriate as part of a coastal garden.

Metal and wood trelliswork is a good material for creating an arbor, the criss-cross pattern ideal for vining plants to thread their branches through. Garden centers and hardware stores sell trellis ready-made.

1

2

1 *Arched grape arbor, Nemours garden, Delaware.* 2 *Columned arbor, Pietermaritzburg, South Africa.* 3 *'Lady banks' rose arbor, Magnolia Plantation, South Carolina.* 4 *Arbor with bench and wall frieze, Hatfield House, UK.* 5 *Sir Edwin Lutyens wall arches, Bois des Moutiers, France.* 6 *Columned arbor, Parry Mansion, California.* 7 *Pergola-style grape arbor, Frederick Garden, Delaware.* 8 *'American Pillar' rose arches, Longwood Gardens, Pennsylvania.*

3

4

6

7

5

8

Perhaps the most famous (and most photographed) garden arch is in Monet's garden. Known as the Grande Allée, it is a walkway 10 ft wide, with six metal arches creating a span 22 ft wide, and 6 ft of space between the gravel walk and the arches for parallel flower borders. At the highest point the arches are 13 ft high. Planted overhead with climbing roses, along the sides with flowering perennials and along the edges with creeping nasturtiums, it creates a flowering tunnel connecting the main house with Monet's water garden and forming an axis on a direct line with the arched Japanese bridge therein. Even the bridge is arched over with a canopy of blue and white wisteria.

Almost any woody plant with pliable branches can be used to create a tunnel-like arbor. At Eleutheran Mills, Delaware, USA, the restored home of the founder of the duPont chemical dynasty, an arched wooden arbor is threaded with apple trees. At the well known British garden of Bodnant, North Wales, yellow-flowering laburnums have been trained over metal frames to form their famous Laburnum Arch, creating a tunnel of gold when it flowers in June.

A common mistake is to provide inadequate strength for arches to support the weight of vines. While sweet autumn clematis and silver fleece vines can be relatively lightweight, their dense knit of stems will trap moisture and soon rot a weak wooden structure, while wisteria, trumpet creeper and kiwi vines can soon become extremely heavy and crush a feeble structure. Once a vine has covered an arch or arbor, rigorous pruning each year may be necessary to keep it from becoming burdensome and weak flowering.

Since arbors are pleasant places to pause, they invariably feature a bench, particularly when the arbor is set into a wall, hedge or cliff. Even simple arches can accommodate a pair of benches aligned to face each other. Arches that are freestanding and designed for walking through often feature a gate. The gate can be useful to keep household dogs from straying into a particular part of the garden, to close off the garden space beyond for any number of reasons, to indicate privacy, and for sheer decorative value.

Long arbors, such as pergolas, don't have to extend in a straight line; they can curve or snake along for added drama. Nor does an arbor always have to be white, though white is a popular color because it stands out well against greenery, and provides a good contrast for most covering vines. Monet's arches for his Grande Allée are painted green, to echo the colors of the house shutters. In gardens where the furniture is painted an indigo blue, an arch of the same color might be appropriate.

1 Rustic arbor, Cedaridge Farm. 2 Clematis and rose-clad arbor, Cedaridge Farm. 3 Yew arch, Bois des Moutiers, France.
4 White wisteria arbor frames a white slatted bench.
5 The laburnum arch, Bodnant, UK. 6 Wall arches, Château de Canon, France. 7 Unadorned pergola-style arbor.
8 Entrance arch with 'Wedding Day' climbing rose.

1

2

3

4

5

6

7

8

Atmospheric effects

1

ATMOSPHERIC EFFECTS The late John Galsworthy, author of *The Forsythe Saga*, declared Magnolia Plantation in South Carolina 'the most beautiful spot in the world, exceeding in beauty even the great romantic Italian gardens of Boboli, Florence and La Mortola, on the Italian Riviera'. The novelist described 'sitting paralyzed by the absurdity of trying to put brush to canvas' in order to paint Magnolia's dream pool with its trellised Long Bridge. What gives Magnolia its great charm is not only its romantic setting within a South Carolina swamp on the banks of the Ashley River, near Charleston, but also a mist that invariably invades the garden each morning, causing the centuries-old oak trees to look ghostly, and the jewel-like flowers of azalea and wisteria to appear muted and dusky.

As the mist clears and the sun appears, the garden becomes alive with shadow contrasts and by the late afternoon the infra-red rays of a sinking sun cause all the colors of the garden to be burnished in reddish tones. When a photography team from a famous camera manufacturer arrived one day to capture the atmospheric romanticism of Magnolia for an advertising poster to be displayed at Grand Central Station, New York City, the mist failed to appear, and so they rented a huge fan from a hardware store, lit a fire and blew the smoke over the ponds to simulate mist! Such is the importance of atmospheric effects in the garden.

It is not surprising, therefore, that today it is possible to purchase a misting device for installation in gardens, with a timer set to blow mist at prescribed intervals. The Grounds for Sculpture Garden, Hamilton, New Jersey, features a hidden mister in its formal water garden, not only to create atmosphere but also to keep plantings of moss alive. One of the reasons Monet decided to make a garden at Giverny was the quality of the light and the tendency for a morning mist to linger in the garden from the nearby River Seine.

Rain, which polishes the bark of trees and stonework and causes enchanting ripples on water, and snow, which can sharpen the outlines of structures and turn the landscape into a harmony of black and white contrasts, are also responsible for beautiful atmospheric effects in the garden. Indeed, the Eskimos have twenty-six words to describe snow, from light dustings that coat the landscape like icing sugar to deep, heavy snows that seem to suffocate the land.

At Cedaridge Farm, which has frequent snowfalls during winter, special attention has been given to areas of the garden for the purpose of looking beautiful under a blanket of snow. This includes the cultivation of grape vines into lofty trees to accentuate sinuous lines against snowy backgrounds, and the placement of several bridges of different styles to enhance the beauty of a meandering stream. Though decorative at any time of year, they look especially romantic when the bridge span and rails are seen against snowy backgrounds.

2

3

1 *Light dusting of snow, Deerfield Garden, Pennsylvania.*
2 *Early morning mist, Magnolia Plantation, South Carolina.*
3 *Monet's water garden in rain.* 4 *Mister wetting stones and moss.* 5 *Ice formation on grasses, Cedaridge Farm.*

4

5

Balconies and balustrades

BALCONIES AND BALUSTRADES Balconies are usually attached to the main residence, sometimes extending from the master bedroom in order to take in a view. However, balconies can also extend from terraces and towers, and create a place to pause and admire the garden from an elevated location. Balconies can be brick, stone, metal or a combination of all three, usually cantilevered out into space to provide a more exhilarating view than from a regular window or door.

In cities like New Orleans, especially the downtown 'French' quarter, ornate metal balconies may run the length of the house to provide a commanding view of the street below, and they may be a feature of every level, crowded with potted plants like Swedish ivy, nasturtiums and periwinkle, spilling decorative foliage down from the balcony like a curtain.

Balustrades are usually rows of balusters, or upright supports, capped by a handrail, ordinarily of stone. From the Italian *balustrata*, balustrades form parapets for terraces and enclose stairways.

1 *French quarter, New Orleans.* 2 *Ivy-leaf geraniums, Swiss chalet.* 3 *Cottage style bedroom balcony.* 4 *Balustrade, Powys Castle, UK.*

1

2

4

3

Basins

BASINS are catchments to hold water, and are mostly made of hollowed-out stone or pottery. In Oriental gardens they serve the practical purpose of providing a sink for washing hands, a pool for birds to bathe, a place to drink spring water, to float a blossom or to catch a reflection. Though basins are most often identified with Oriental gardens, they also feature in European designs. One of the most exquisite is at the Villa Lante, near Rome, where a long stone banquet table features a wine-cooling trough in the middle. In European gardens of the 17th and 18th century, it became fashionable to have lead cisterns to catch rainwater for supplemental irrigation, and these basins formed a decorative element.

In Oriental gardens, the most valued type of basin is natural stone, hollowed by weather to form a water-holding depression. Japanese basins for drinking are often filled by hand, with a ladle nearby, but more usual is the use of a bamboo spout that drips water continuously, allowing the basin to overflow imperceptibly, and water a surrounding mossy area.

1 Dish-shaped basin balanced on stones. 2 Oriental-style basin in Japanese garden. 3 Low stone basin provides drinking water for pets. 4 Rectangular basin incorporated into a ruin.
5 Lead cistern catches water from a wall fountain.

Beds and borders

BEDS AND BORDERS are good display spaces for featuring plants, generally in an assortment of kinds and colors. A bed is usually an island of soil, in a variety of shapes, including square, rectangular, round, oval and kidney-shaped. Geometric-shaped beds are especially popular in sunken gardens where the entrance provides an elevated view of the formal design. Borders are usually straight or curved and have a backdrop – generally a wall, a fence or a hedge.

While island beds in parks and public places have been popular for growing annuals and bulbs for centuries, the British plantsman, Alan Bloom, made the displaying of perennials in island beds popular by using them extensively at the family's show gardens in Bressingham, Norfolk. Most of the Bressingham island beds are kidney-shaped and display three tiers of color – low, spreading plants for edging, tall plants for the center, and intermediate height plants in between.

Borders generally confine tall plants to the back, with intermediate height plants in front of them, and low spreading plants along the edge. Borders can feature all annuals, all perennials, or all shrubs (a shrubbery), or the plants can be mixed. Gertrude Jekyll advocated designing mixed borders for peak color during a particular season, and she liked to orchestrate color so that hot colors merged into cool colors, and then changed to hot colors again. If she saw gaps of faded foliage before the end of the season she would prune back

1

2

1 *Island beds filled with tulips, Keukenhof, Holland.*
2 *Parterre beds filled with annuals, colonial garden, Philadelphia.* 3 *Mixed perennial border, Glencoe Farm, Pennsylvania.*

3

1

the dead leaves and replace them with annuals in pots, so the borders always looked filled with color.

At Cedaridge Farm all new flowerbeds and borders are dug to a depth of at least two feet, and since the indigenous soil is heavy clay, the soil is piled onto a tarp. Perennials are greedy feeders, so in addition to adding compost and sand, a granular high-phosphorus fertilizer (good for root development and flower production) is mixed in thoroughly. When the resulting improved soil mix is returned to the bed, the fluffed-up soil will extend above the surrounding soil level, providing improved drainage. Additional feeding is done at the start of each spring season. Granular fertilizer is raked into the upper soil surface, or else a soil drench of liquid fertilizer is applied.

Perennials can look most dramatic in double borders, especially straight parallel borders that are divided by a grass or flagstone path. With this formal layout it's possible to then feature an interesting focal point at the end of the path, such as a statue or a gazebo.

Between Monet's house and his Clos Normand flower garden is a series of island beds that change with the seasons – tulips for spring, followed by bedding geraniums for summer. They act as a transition between his porch and the heart of the flower garden. One of the island beds features everblooming pink standard roses, 'Centennaire de Lourdes', to create a pink and red color harmony when the geraniums bloom.

2

1 Island beds with geraniums and rose standards, Monet's garden. 2 Perennial border at Waterperry garden, UK. 3 Summer bulbs and annuals in a Christchurch park, New Zealand. 4 Exotic border at Chanticleer garden, Pennsylvania.

3

4

Benches

BENCHES A garden without benches is like a theater without a stage, and it is rare that you find a garden without one. A very famous large garden in Normandy, Le Vasterival – established by Princess Greta Sturdza – is completely devoid of benches, but that is because she conducts a lot of tours around her property, and she wants nothing to cause visitors to dawdle and put her behind schedule.

Benches are not only good places to pause and take in a view. They can be decorative ornaments to admire at the end of a vista or along a path, and they can help establish the theme or period of a garden more successfully than plants alone. There are lots of bench styles, and some are so distinctive that they identify a particular garden. For example, in the grounds of Versailles, Claude Monet found an all-wooden bench to copy that has become a trademark of his garden. Painted apple green and featuring a curved seat and curved slatted backrest, it can accommodate six people with ease and is now widely advertised as the 'Monet bench' in mail-order catalogs. Giverny's first benches of this type were probably made at the palace's woodworking shop in Versailles.

It was perhaps the Victorians more than anyone else who popularized benches. They had a love affair with anything Greek or Roman and so many benches of the period are ornate granite or marble structures that might seem at home in a Mediterranean ruin as much as a garden. The Victorian fascination for stonework was so strong that even rustic benches were made from cement designed to simulate tree branches. The Edwardians, by contrast, liked metal benches, and the famous iron foundry at Coalbrookdale, in Shropshire, turned out more than forty designs including benches that

1 *Slab stone bench, Oehme Alpine Gardens, Washington State.*
2 *Slatted teak bench with an elevated view.* 3 *Spanish-style bench with tile backrest.* 4 *Metal bench with grape vine design.*

1

3

4

resembled fern fronds and bramble vines. Though these are the least comfortable to sit on, they are often the most charming to view, and they seem to look especially attractive in herb gardens.

Other metal benches are built for extreme comfort, the rods rolled into smooth flat strips, then bent into the contours of the body. However, all-metal benches as a whole can overheat on hot days and feel chilly to sit on during cold days (stone benches, too), and so the combination of iron-and-wood, using wooden slats for the seat and cast-iron for the ends and arm rests, became popular – a style exemplified by the famous 'Charleston Battery' bench, which can be seen everywhere in the historic district of Charleston, South Carolina. The great French Impressionist painters loved to paint a similar bench found extensively in French parks in the 1800s. This was long and sleek with many dark green slats, capable of seating four people. Another park bench favored by the Impressionists had ornate metal arm-rests contoured to look like grape vines, and wooden slats for the seats.

When choosing a place to sit in the garden, consider the idea of creating an exhedra – a circular space with three sets of benches facing each other. There are two exhedras in Monet's garden: one with curved wooden benches on a circle of gravel in the flower garden and another in his water garden, where white stone benches sit on a circle of gravel screened by bamboo. The purpose of an exhedra is to provide a place for a group of people to sit intimately outdoors and discuss business, politics or family matters.

1

3

2

1 Cement slave bench, Stellenberg garden, Capetown. 2 Teak bench on cobblestones. 3 French park bench and matching side tables. 4 Teak bench surrounding a tree. 5 Wooden slab bench, Magnolia Plantation, South Carolina. 6 Ecclesiastical bench, Carmel Mission, California. 7 American colonial bench, Williamsburg. 8 Lutyens-style bench facing a reflecting pool.

4

8

7

6

5

When choosing a bench it is not only important to obtain the right design in keeping with the style of the garden, but also to ensure that it is the right scale, taking into consideration its surroundings. Rustic benches made from driftwood and woven willow branches can look right for informal gardens, but in a large, formal area, such as the termination of a rectangular reflecting pool, a substantial Lutyens bench might be more suitable. Solidly made of teak, the most durable and weather-resistant of wood, it features a Chippendale design backrest and scrolled armrests, the legs braced by crossbeams. Designed by Sir Edwin Lutyens, it is one of the most substantial and costliest of garden benches.

Bench design allows for unusual creativity. At Colonial Williamsburg there is a beautiful bench incorporated into the fence rail of a wooden footbridge, and at the Oehme Alpine Gardens, Washington State, there is a stone bench carved into the face of a gigantic boulder, the branches of a weeping spruce softening the stone backdrop and thyme planted around the base so that when bruised by feet a spicy aroma pervades the air. A number of New Zealand gardens feature benches made from metal tractor wheels, while several British estates feature 'wheelbarrow' benches with handles at one end and a wheel at the other so they can be moved easily. Swing benches suspended from tree limbs are popular in coastal gardens, while Adirondack benches with steeply inclined seats seem to look especially attractive in front of a mountain view or beside a lake.

1 *High-backed wooden bench, Innisfree garden, New York State.* 2 *Charleston Battery bench.* 3 *Rustic wooden bench with cartwheel backrest.* 4 *English Regency-style metal bench, Cedaridge Farm.*

Birds, bees and butterflies

BIRDS, BEES AND BUTTERFLIES Although birds are an essential part of gardens whether they are wild or domesticated, they can be a nuisance. For instance, it is delightful to tour a garden early in the morning, with mist rising off a pond, to see a blue heron standing statuesque in ambush for frogs; but what a disappointment it can be to find that it has eaten all the koi and goldfish as though they were breadcrumbs! The mating displays of male peacocks, as they fan out their iridescent feathers, can be beautiful, but their raucous cries in the early morning can bring complaints from neighbors, and what damage they can do to newly planted flowerbeds! Waterbirds like swans and geese, though beautiful to see swimming across lakes and ponds, can become aggressive during the nesting season and scare visitors, while the droppings of geese can be unsightly.

Aside from the above, the presence of birds can greatly enhance the enjoyment of a garden, and populations of songbirds in particular should be encouraged by setting up nesting boxes, bird feeders and birdbaths, since they can help keep insect pests in check.

Before introducing exotic birds (like parrots, fantail doves and flamingoes) be sure you can provide sufficient shelter during cold periods, and that the climate will encourage their survival. If a shelter is needed, give thought to making it a decorative element in the landscape. Aviaries for housing collections of tropical birds like parakeets and exotic pheasants are popular in subtropical and tropical gardens, especially when disguised to look like gazebos.

Perhaps the most appropriate presence of a bird in a garden is at Maple Glen, in the South Island of New Zealand. In an area where both the giant moa and smaller bush moa once roamed by the thousands, and became extinct after Maori occupation of the islands, the owners have introduced friendly emus. While not as big as a giant moa, they resemble a bush moa, and their presence in the garden is enchanting.

Take special care when choosing nesting boxes. Wrens, for example, like boxes with tiny holes they can squeeze into but are too small for starlings to gain entry. Nesting boxes for small birds like wrens and bluetits should not have a perch in front of the hole otherwise a predatory jay might be able to balance on it and stretch a leg inside to grab eggs or young. Nesting boxes on poles should have a cone-shaped metal shield below the box so that rats cannot scale the pole and steal eggs.

Dovecotes and pigeon roosts have been part of gardens and landscapes since the Persians built special circular stone towers with nesting holes to house thousands of pigeons as

1

2   3

1 Peacock displays iridescent feathers. 2 Dovecote with fantail doves. 3 Bird box made from discarded boot. 4 Pair of swans, Maple Glen garden, New Zealand.

4

food, starting around 3000 BC. From there the towers spread to Egypt, Europe and Britain's far-flung colonies. In France the fantail dove was especially prized for both food and ornamental value because of its snow-white coloration, melodious cooing song, and habit of fanning its tail. Historical dovecotes housing more than a thousand birds are still common in France and the British Isles. Today, few new dovecote towers are being built because of the popularity and low cost of chicken, but many gardens feature decorative wooden communal dovecotes on pedestals as focal points in herb and perennial gardens.

Apiaries are homes for bees. One, or a line of beehives in sunlight, can serve the practical purpose of providing lots of honeybees for pollinating plants, especially fruiting kinds and orchard varieties, and they are a source of delicious honey. Beehives can provide a decorative accent away from paths and seating areas where wayward bees can cause distress to visitors. The most common form of beehive is a box-like structure on legs, and a hinged lid that is slanted to shed rain. More decorative designs are also available, including the popular beeskep – a domed weave of wickerwork that looks especially attractive as an accent in herb gardens. Those made from woven wattles can look most appealing and are more durable than wickerwork.

Butterflies are welcome in gardens, for they provide flickering movement and pollination. The easiest way to attract them is to plant flowering annuals with strong colors, like red, yellow and blue, including marigolds, zinnias, asters and echium, also specific food plants for the caterpillar larvae to feed upon, such as milkweed (*Asclepias*) for monarchs and Queen Anne's lace (*Daucus*) for swallowtails. Flowers of summer-flowering butterfly bush (*Buddleja davidii*), perennial *Sedum spectabile* and the perennial butterfly weed (*Asclepias tuberosa*) contain nectar as food for all kinds of butterflies.

1 *Indigo blue dovecote with rat-proof overhang.*
2 *Captive flamingoes at Garden of the Groves, Bahamas.*
3 *Pet emu at Maple Glen garden, New Zealand.* 4 *French-style stone dovecote with peaked roof.* 5 *Swallowtail butterfly on zinnia.* 6 *Decorative beehive in an herb garden.*

Boardwalks

BOARDWALKS are raised walkways. They are good to consider for garden terrain unsuitable for a footpath – for example, to cross a section of boggy soil, an expanse of shallow water, uneven rocky ground or an area of raised tree roots.

Sections of boardwalk extend miles through wildlife preserves, including the Swamp Garden at Magnolia Plantation, South Carolina. There, the boardwalk takes visitors over shallow water, providing them with an elevated view of basking alligators and nesting egrets. Many coastal gardens will feature boardwalks to cross a section of sand dunes, providing comfortable access from the main house to the beach.

For safety reasons, boardwalks should have rails, and where they extend long distances they should meander and occasionally widen out into observation platforms, preferably with a bench to rest. They can be made to look rustic by placing the boards in a random width design. Wildlife observation towers and tree-houses can also be placed at strategic points for visitors to gain an even higher elevated view of the surrounding area.

Cedaridge Farm features a short section of boardwalk in combination with a flat wooden bridge span. The boardwalk crosses a swampy area, while the bridge spans a narrow stream, at the same time elevating visitors into the branches of wild plum blossom that flowers in April, followed by edible plums.

1 *Japanese-style zig-zag boardwalk over water, Missouri Botanical Garden.* 2 *Staggered boardwalk across boggy soil in a Japanese garden.* 3 *Arched footbridge and boardwalk negotiate boggy soil.* 4 *Boardwalk elevated into tree canopy.* 5 *Boardwalk through sandy nature preserve, Long Island, New York State.*

1

2

5

4

3

Boats and boathouses

BOATS AND BOATHOUSES Since lakes and ponds are often an important feature of gardens, boats are frequently part of the visual drama of these water features. The Japanese often leave a boat tethered to a mooring line out in the water as a place for fish to hide from predatory hawks and herons. Perhaps the most familiar boat used as a garden ornament is the sleek, green rowboat used by Claude Monet to paint from the middle of his pond, and itself a favorite motif in his paintings.

With a boat there is usually a boat dock or a boathouse. Although Monet's water garden was too small to feature a boathouse, it does have a dock – a flight of concrete steps arched over by climbing roses. The steps curve out into the water, allowing easy access to the rowboat. More often, boat docks are wooden jetties that extend out from the shore for a boat to tie alongside. Boathouses feature in Oriental gardens, and are not only places to provide shelter for the craft but may also feature a docking platform with steps.

Small boats can be recycled as planters, and up-ended to form an instant tool shed, both appropriate features for coastal gardens. Boats as sculpture feature extravagantly at the Italianate garden of Villa Viscaya, Miami, Florida, where a massive stone galleon creates an island for entertaining. In the Vatican Gardens, Rome, an elaborate metal galleon spouts numerous water jets vertically and horizontally, as a symbol of the Vatican's world-wide influence.

1 *Boathouse and lake at Bodnant, Wales.* 2 *Dinghy used to store tools, Stewart Island, New Zealand.* 3 *Galleon fountain, Vatican Gardens.* 4 *Monet's distinctive green rowboat.* 5 *Bamboo boathouse, Shugakuin Imperial Villa, Kyoto.*

Bog and swamp gardens

BOG AND SWAMP GARDENS have the potential to make the most beautiful of all garden spaces because three tiers of plants can be employed here to work design magic. First, a bog needs moisture-laden soil so plants that like their feet wet, such as bog primulas and pitcher plants (*Sarracenia*) can form healthy colonies. Second, a bog generally benefits from a pond or a stream as a central focal point, and so floating plants like waterlilies can be considered. Then the area surrounding the boggy soil – ground elevated above the bog – can be filled with plants that thrive in the atmosphere of a bog, but in moderately well-drained soil, such as astilbe, rodgersias and hostas. A host of structures can also be used to make bog gardens appealing. These include stepping stones, bridges, and boardwalks. When all three environmental conditions – bog, water and dry ground – are planted appropriately, the effect can be exceedingly colorful, extending through all the seasons.

Be aware, however, that certain desirable bog-loving plants can be extremely aggressive, and so a bog garden can mean high maintenance, keeping wayward plants within bounds. Ostrich ferns, cat-tails (*Typha*) and flag irises in particular will quickly spread into areas with weaker plants, such as candelabra primulas and pitcher plants, and suffocate them.

Nowhere in the world are bog gardens more skillfully planted than in Scotland, the US Pacific Northwest coast, and New Zealand, where a mostly cool climate and high rainfall favors

1 *Bog-loving 'Inschriach' candelabra hybrid primulas.* 2 *Bog-tolerant snakeweed blooms in late spring.* 3 *Colony of pitcher plants beside a stream, Clos Coudray, France.* 4 *Boardwalk traversing an alligator-infested swamp garden, Magnolia Plantation, South Carolina.*

the planting of bog gardens using bold plant accents, especially tree ferns, yellow skunk cabbage (*Lysichiton americanus*) and Chilean gunnera (*Gunnera tinctoria*).

Swamp gardens are generally larger in size than bog gardens, which can be as small as a bath tub. Two especially beautiful swamp gardens exist near Charleston, South Carolina, in a section of coastal plain known as the Low Country. They are found at Magnolia Plantation and Cypress Gardens. Though Magnolia's 500 acres includes woodland surrounding several lakes, the plantation was carved out of a cypress swamp, and today features a special alligator-infested swamp garden, where indigenous wildflowers and waterbirds are encouraged to thrive. A snaking boardwalk allows visitors to traverse the swamp in comfort. Nearby Cypress Gardens is also located in a cypress swamp, with a raised footpath taking visitors across the swamp and around a series of connecting lakes. Boat tours even take visitors through the swamp so that colonies of native swamp wildflowers and wildlife can be observed closely.

1 *Bog-loving* Primula helodoxa, *Pukeiti garden, New Zealand.* 2 *Wooden pavers keep feet dry in Clos Coudray bog garden, France.* 3 *Arched wooden bridge spans a stream at Attadale garden, Scotland.* 4 *Bog garden with arum lilies and Bowles golden grass at Airlies garden, New Zealand.*

1

2

3

4

Bonsai

BONSAI is the art of training and restricting a tree's roots with the aid of a shallow container known as a bonsai dish so the plant stays dwarfed. There is also an art to the pruning and shaping of the plant to create the illusion of a mature specimen, especially one that has been affected by harsh weather so that twisted branches and a gnarled trunk give the impression of venerable age.

Evergreen conifers such as pines, spruce and juniper are especially popular bonsai subjects because in the wild they cling to cracks in precipitous cliffs and produce a naturalistic, sculptural quality. Deciduous trees like ginkgo and Japanese maple are also popular because of their interesting leaf shapes and bright autumn leaf colours.

Though most people consider bonsai to be good for indoor decoration, they can be displayed outdoors to create a beautiful focal point, displayed on pedestals at the center of a Japanese-style courtyard, in a wall niche or beside a waterfall. In areas with harsh winters, outdoor bonsai should be moved indoors to a frost-free location since the shallow bonsai containers offer little protection from freezing.

For an especially attractive display, consider growing bonsai on a boulder, such as lightweight tufa, with a planting hole chiseled out of the rock to accommodate the roots.

1 Bonsai Japanese maple in autumn colors. 2 Bonsai pine in a Japanese garden. 3 Ancient bonsai juniper with reed background. 4 Bonsai collection, Rosade Bonsai Studio, Pennsylvania.

1

2

3

4

Boulders and story stones

BOULDERS AND STORY STONES Boulders can feature in gardens as a monolith (a single block of stone) or as a grouping to create a natural sculptural element, or they can be arranged to create a natural-looking rock fall, perhaps with a trickle of water coursing down them. If a garden already has a prominent boulder, especially one that is massive, immovable and solid-looking, it should be used as the dominant feature in a landscape to create a dramatic focal point. However, the late Katsuo Saito, a notable Japanese landscape architect, made an interesting observation about boulders in the landscape: 'Though a naked woman is beautiful, if she is covered in some thin veiling, her beauty is greatly enhanced. A boulder, partially concealed by foliage or moss, presents the same sensation.'

Oriental garden designers prefer to choose one exceptional boulder as a focal point, rather than a cluster of mediocre ones. Boulders that symbolize animals are highly prized and given names like 'owl rock' and 'rock of the yawning lion'. Also highly prized are boulders with richly textured surfaces, because stone that is pitted and pock-marked, with crevices, hollows and fractures, symbolizes antiquity.

Chinese gardens in particular feature 'sculptural' boulders, some of the most highly valued taken from the bottom of T'ai Hu Lake in Suzhou, where storms and the forces of water have fashioned limestone into amazing shapes.

Story stones in the garden have been brought into national prominence as a result of Ian Hamilton Finlay, the Scottish artist, using them at Little Sparta. These are stone slabs engraved with messages, sometimes whimsical, to make people pause and think or smile. Others provide a memorial to an event Finlay wishes to commemorate, such as the sinking of a ship. Story stones can be placed at the entrance to a garden, and as surprise elements beside wandering paths. At Winterthur garden, Delaware, a series of story stones resembles a miniature Stonehenge in a children's garden known as The Enchanted Woods. Ruins are also good places to feature story stones.

1 *Clusters of boulders, Ford Rock Garden, Vail, Colorado.*
2 *Boulder accent beside flagstone path.* 3 *Stone mile marker used as moss garden accent.* 4 *Tilted boulder accent framed by sinuous Japanese maple branches.* 5 *Story stones within a ruin at Chanticleer garden, Pennsylvania.* 6 *Oriental style rock garden, Innisfree garden, New York State.*

Bridges

BRIDGES need not always cross a water feature such as a pond or stream. In Oriental gardens especially, bridges are used to span stone-filled depressions that recreate a dry riverbed.

Of all structural accents in a garden, bridges offer the greatest diversity of design, and splendid opportunities for originality. Indeed, a special design – like the white trellised Long Bridge at Magnolia Plantation, South Carolina – can look so distinctive it establishes a romantic aura for a garden, and the bridge becomes a trademark, readily identifying that historic garden.

Another distinctive, easily identified bridge is Monet's green, canopied, arched Japanese footbridge, spanning a corner of his Giverny water garden. Monet originally painted the arched bridge white to accentuate its water reflection, but later made it green and added a canopy to support vines of blue and white wisteria. When the vines bloom, in early May, they drape their long flower panicles below the canopy, creating a lace curtain effect, and adding a shimmering sensation to that part of the garden.

Bridges can be strategically placed to provide an elevated view, especially if the span is arched, allowing a splendid prospect of a pond, stream or lake during the day, and the moon's reflection at night. While flat spans are the easiest to

1

1 Monet's wisteria-covered Japanese bridge. 2 Wooden bridge incorporating a bench. 3 Corn crib bridge at Innisfree garden, New York State. 4 The Long Bridge, Magnolia Plantation, South Carolina.

2

3

4

1

install and the easiest to negotiate, unless they are raised on posts with steps leading on and off the raised section, they don't have the commanding presence that an arched span can provide. Care must be taken with arched bridges to ensure that the arch is not too steep to negotiate in wet weather. The arch of Monet's bridge has raised wooden batons that act like steps. Higher arched bridges – especially those popular in Chinese gardens – will even feature actual steps to make it easier to step up and off the steep ends of the arch.

To ensure that a bridge does not wobble, the ends of the bridge should rest on a firm foundation – preferably concrete – although short spans can have boards resting on packed soil or crushed stone. Handrails are also advisable for long, narrow spans for safety reasons.

Though wood is the most economical building material for bridges, metal and stone bridges can be considered. Arched stone bridges, like those found in desolate sections of Scotland and the Yorkshire Moors, can look sensational in informal gardens. Moreover, the walkways of stone bridges can be covered in turf for a more natural, restful look.

1 *Stone hump-back bridge, Glenfalloch garden, New Zealand.*
2 *Monet-style bridge painted blue, Hortensia garden, New Zealand.* 3 *Combination metal and wood bridge, Cedaridge Farm.*

2

3

Bulb gardens

BULB GARDENS The world's most elaborately planted bulb garden is Keukenhof, near Amsterdam. A showplace for the Dutch bulb industry, the formal and informal 'idea gardens' rely almost exclusively on spring-flowering bulbs for colorful impact, especially tulips, a plant family that has the most extensive color range in horticulture, with the exception of orchids. This three-month spring extravaganza draws more than a million visitors a year. The tulips grown at Keukenhof are classified as early, mid-season and late, and though individually the flowers rarely last more than two weeks, there is enough diversity to keep a continuous parade of color from early March to the end of May, supported by daffodils, hyacinths, crown imperials, and a host of 'minor' bulbs like grape hyacinths, Spanish bluebells and anemones. Though many of the highly bred tulips will not come back in successive years, daffodils generally will. Other spring-flowering bulbs that will naturalize freely include snowdrops, winter aconites, English bluebells and Siberian squill.

1 *Formal bulb planting, Keukenhof, Holland.* 2 *Partnership of lily-flowered tulips and crown imperials.* 3 *Shaded parterre garden with tulips, Virginia House, Virginia.* 4 *Pink-and-blue color harmony, Monet's garden, using blue forget-me-nots and cottage tulips.*

1

Spring-flowering bulbs can be combined with annuals, perennials and shrubs to intensify the color impact of mixed flower borders, especially in English cottage gardens. Bluebells beneath orange, yellow or pink azaleas can make a particularly attractive plant partnership.

In addition to spring-flowering bulbs, which are planted in the autumn for flowering the following spring, there are summer and autumn-flowering kinds that are best planted in spring. Summer-flowering bulbs like dahlias, gladiolus, also the tuberous begonias and dahlias, are not generally hardy and must be replanted each season. These types can be lifted in autumn and stored in a dark, frost-free location. Among hardy summer-flowering bulbs are garden lilies and the small naked ladies (*Lycoris squamigera*). Autumn-flowering bulbs like colchicum, allium and saffron crocus are best planted in drifts on sunny slopes, at the edge of woodland and in rock gardens.

Most bulbs like good drainage, and to maintain perennial bloom, feeding twice a year is advisable – a high phosphorus fertilizer applied to the soil before the plants bloom in spring, and again in autumn after frost. Exceptions to the good drainage rule are summer-flowering calla lilies (*Zantedeschia*) and cannas, both of which thrive in boggy soil.

2

1 *Dried seed heads of giant allium.* **2** *Colchicums naturalized, Cedaridge Farm.* **3** *Tulips and grape hyacinths planted informally among trees.* **4** *Woodland daffodil display, Cedaridge Farm.*

3

4

Chinese gardens

CHINESE GARDENS Since the first century, Chinese gardens have been greatly influenced by Buddhism. As early as 612, a garden designer named Roji-no-Takumi erected a miniature mountain landscape as the symbolic representation of Sumeru, the mythical mountain located in the middle of the Buddhist universe.

Other Buddhist gardens have attempted to create perceptions of the 'The Pure Land', which was described as a garden of beautiful pavilions overlooking spacious ponds, filled with lotus blossoms. Here the souls of believers dwelled in bliss, surrounded by the fragrance of flowers and the sounds of celestial music.

The Chinese word for landscape is *shan shu*, meaning 'mountains and water', and in Chinese concepts of harmony and tranquillity they represent Yin and Yang, the mountains representing maleness and the water female symbolism. The Chinese consider these to be complementary opposites, or perfect balance. In traditional Chinese gardens, therefore, the principal components are rocks introduced to look like mountainous landscapes, and water, in the form of a carp pond and running streams. Plants are incidental, introduced sparingly to emphasize complementary structural qualities, such as the assertiveness of erect bamboo canes for maleness, contrasting with the submissive floating pads of waterlilies for the female counterpart.

Balance, therefore, is the key to understanding ancient Chinese garden design. It is also key to an understanding of Japanese garden design, though the Japanese refined it even further, tempering the ostentation to create a landscape still full of symbolism.

Water in the form of rain, frost, snow and mist is an important consideration of Chinese garden design. The Emperor Kao-ts'ung, of the Ch'ing dynasty, is said to have once made a special trip to an island garden, known as The Garden of the Mists for the prevalence of coastal mist that imbued it with muted light and made the stonework shine like polished ebony. The mist also stimulated luxurious green moss growth. On his visit the Emperor was disappointed when the sun shone brilliantly, bleaching out the saturated colors, and the mist failed to appear.

Wang Wei (AD 699–759), a poet, painter and statesman, left a remarkable scroll painting to show what early Chinese garden design looked like. Widowed in his early thirties, he created a garden for his mother in an area of rugged hills, lakes and streams near Ch'ang-an, and after her death bequeathed it to a nearby Buddhist monastery. We know about the garden from his scroll painting that depicts what garden historians today call a 'stroll garden', whereby a labyrinth of paths takes visitors on a visual adventure along a shoreline, beneath cliffs, criss-crossing streams, and through hidden valleys to individual garden spaces, called 'cups', that invariably include a focal point for introspection, each focal accent enclosed by a screening hedge, fence, wall or grove of woody plants.

1 *Pavilion, Sun Yat Sen Garden, Vancouver.* 2 *Buddha framed by bamboo, Cypress Gardens, Florida.* 3 *Stone arch with spirit stone, Innisfree garden, New York State.* 4 *Boulder accent, Innisfree garden.* 5 *Moongate framing stone pillars, Chinese Scholar's Garden, Staten Island, New York State.* 6 *Zig-zag bridge, Chinese Scholar's Garden.*

Coastal gardens

COASTAL GARDENS that allow visitors glimpses of the sea as they stroll garden paths, like Tresco Abbey Gardens in the Isles of Scilly, and Inverewe Garden, in Scotland, are among the world's most beautiful. They are also the most difficult to establish. When located close to the shoreline, coastal gardens must contend with high winds and salt pollution, impoverished sandy soils and dry spells. Shelter from high winds can be achieved by planting wind and salt-resistant hedges, such as Monterey pine or Monterey cypress. Sandy soil can be improved by adding loads of compost, and dry spells can be endured through the installation of an irrigation system. Once these factors are in place the results can be phenomenal, since many plants relish the cool temperatures, morning mists and air circulation of a coastal location.

Though Tresco and Inverewe are large gardens beyond the means of most people, the small-space coastal garden of poet Celia Thaxter, off the coast of New Hampshire, was made world famous by a book she wrote, entitled *An Island Garden* (1894, facsimile reprint, 1988). The book is illustrated by evocative watercolor paintings of American Impressionist artist Childe Hassam. These show the 15 ft wide by 50 ft long cutting garden filled with annuals, especially poppies and hollyhocks. Though the clapboard house that immediately overlooked the garden perished in a fire, the garden itself has been restored and is open to the public, accessible by ferry from Portsmouth, New Hampshire.

Coastal erosion can be a threat from high tides and high winds, and so terracing may be necessary, even using wooden boards if stone seawalls are cost prohibitive. Where sand dunes exist, the shifting sand can bury plantings, but species that stabilize shifting sand can be established, including marram grass, rugosa roses, iceplants and hottentot fig.

Good structures to consider for coastal gardens include observation decks facing the sea, a gazebo or whale-watch tower, a boardwalk to provide comfortable access to the shoreline, driftwood accents for ornamental value, even fences made from driftwood. Boulders, bleached bones, ship's figureheads, anchors, lobster pots and buoys can be used also as decorative elements to capture a feeling of the sea.

1

2

3

4

1 *Matai Moana coastal garden, New Zealand.* 2 *Buoy garden accent, Shetland, UK.* 3 *Whale skeleton and wreck beach accents, Bitter End Yacht Club, Virgin Gorda.*
4 *Shirley poppies, Celia Thaxter Garden, Maine.* 5 *Terraces, Inverewe garden, Scotland.* 6 *Hydrangeas, Port Blanc, Britanny.*
7 *Mixed annuals, Sooke Harbour House, Vancouver Island.*

5

6

7

Cold frames and cloches

COLD FRAMES AND CLOCHES are highly practical structures for the garden, but in many gardens little thought is given to improve their utilitarian appearance. Similarly, glass tent cloches and recycled plastic gallon milk containers are used for protecting tender transplants from frost, in spite of the fact that more decorative bell jars and lead-paned lantern cloches can vastly improve the decorative look of a vegetable garden.

Though cold frames are essential to harden off seedlings before transplanting them to the garden, and not considered particularly attractive, these structures can be used to force tender plants to bloom early. The resulting riot of color is certainly not deserving of being hidden from view behind a shed or hedge. Inca lilies (*Alstromeria*), African agapanthus, Persian ranunculus and French anemones that are not reliably frost hardy will often overwinter in unheated cold frames to bloom extra early in the season. Also, cloches used to protect plants at the beginning of the season can act as a 'frost extender' at the end of the season to protect compact vegetable varieties like lettuce and bush beans.

Terracotta forcing pots are also used in vegetable gardens to force rhubarb and kale into early sprouting. Bulbous in shape, resembling olive jars, but open at the bottom so they can be placed over dormant roots to provide warmth and darkness, they are highly decorative. At the Lost Gardens of Heligan, Cornwall, a large collection of forcing pots is grouped near a potting shed as a decorative element.

1 *Cold frame and solar-heated greenhouse, Longwood Gardens, Pennsylvania.* 2 *Rhubarb forcing pots, Heligan garden, UK.* 3 *Lantern cloch, Cedaridge Farm.* 4 *Hinged window frames provide good air circulation on hot days.*

1

2

4
3

Color theme gardens

COLOR THEME GARDENS The great Victorian plants-woman Gertrude Jekyll wrote that it's not enough to have a collection of plants haphazardly planted without thought to pleasing combinations such as color harmonies. Pleasing color themes can be *monochromatic* (shades and tones of one color such as pink, red, crimson), two *complementary* colors (opposites on the color wheel such as yellow and violet), two *analogous* colors (adjacent colors on a color wheel such as yellow and orange), *triadic combinations* (equidistant on the color wheel such as red, yellow and blue), or *polychromatic* (multiple colors).

As well as paying attention to petal colors, a color harmony should take background colors into consideration, such as a red entrance door, blue house siding, a dark hemlock hedge, a stretch of blue water, or a bright green meadow. The Impressionist painter Claude Monet filled his garden with color harmonies, and when he painted his garden with people in it, he even color coordinated their clothing to complement the flower and foliage colors – an idea that did not occur to Miss Jekyll, as she always dressed in black. She didn't particularly like single color (monochromatic) plantings, but preferred to plant in two or more contrasting colors. She also liked color echoes, such as along perennial borders where she might start with cool colors like blue and mauve, merge into hot colors like red, orange and yellow, then return again to the cool colors.

1 *Silver garden, Auckland Botanic Gardens, Manurewa, New Zealand.* 2 *Yellow-and-orange garden, Ladew Topiary Garden, Maryland.* 3 *Hot color harmony from English wallflowers, Monet's garden.*

1

2

3

Monochromatic plantings that feature plants of a single pure color are generally boring, with the exception of red because green foliage actually makes it a complementary color harmony, red and green being opposites on the color wheel. One of the most popular monochromatic color-theme gardens is an all-white planting, made popular by the writer Vita Sackville-West at her home, Sissinghurst Castle, in the south of England. There, in a special walled garden area she used not only white flowers such as white rambler roses and white calla lilies, but also cream-colored flowers like feverfew and plants with silver foliage, like artemisia.

At Cedaridge Farm, an all-white garden of mostly fragrant white flowers creates a beautiful evening garden, within view of a conservatory which also serves as a dining alcove. (For more information on evening gardens, see page 73.)

The complementary color harmonies yellow and violet and blue and orange are so similar they can be used inter-changeably – yellow and blue and orange and violet. These pairings were all popular with Claude Monet. Since green is the color of foliage, he made his red and green pairings more appealing by using pink flowers among the red (for example, pink and red tulips), and he added silver as an edging by using the silvery leaves of dianthus. The idea of this silver, green, red and pink combination came to him while out walking one day. He spotted a field of red and pink poppies on a green hill-side, with silvery wild sage in the background, a motif which he painted and then adapted to his garden.

Analogous color harmonies usually consist of two or three colors, for example yellow, orange and red, which are the components of Claude Monet's famous 'hot color plantings'. He also used blue, violet and mauve to create 'cool color plantings'.

A triadic color harmony popular with Monet involves blue, pink and white. He liked to plant this combination in shady areas, using shade-loving plants like pansies and violas. He also considered blue alone a good color for shade, as he thought blue enhanced shadows better than any other color,

1

8

7

1 Yellow-and-blue theme using yellow loosestrife and blue veronica. 2 Blue wisteria and California lilac create a monochromatic blue color theme. 3 Hot color harmony using yellow loosestrife and orange, red and yellow Asiatic lilies, Monet's garden. 4 A predominantly orange and black garden. 5 All-pink monochromatic garden involving pink azaleas and pink Judas trees, Cedaridge Farm. 6 Blue and yellow color harmony involving mostly blue violas and campanula, and yellow marigolds and snapdragons. 7 Red garden using tulips and tree peonies. 8 Polychromatic planting of bearded irises.

hence the preponderance of blue forget-me-nots and bluebells in woodland areas around his pond.

The most difficult color combinations to achieve are polychromatic, where a lot of distinct colors compete for attention. This can look garish, except when a single plant genus is used for the rainbow effect, such as bearded irises, primroses and pansies, all of which have an unusually wide color range, including black.

When striving to create a color theme, don't just consider the color of flower petals, but also foliage effects. Bronze smoke bush (*Cotinus coggygria*), silver Russian olive, yellow false cypresses, blue spruce and red blood grass (*Imperata cylindrical* 'Red Baron') are examples of trees, shrubs and grasses with unusual foliage colors as colorful as any flower. When foliage colors alone are used to color a landscape, it is known as a tapestry garden.

A French chemist, Michel Eugene Chevreuil, was the first to describe the laws of colors and to publish a color wheel. He even suggested ways of applying the laws of colors to the garden, and subsequently two French garden writers – J. Decaisne and C. Naudin – elaborated on Chevreuil's theories in their series *Manual de l'amateur du jardin* (1862–1891). Most importantly, they explained the vital role of white in the landscape, for they discovered that white will enliven any color next to which it is placed, like the white centers of blue delphiniums and red lupins. Possibly it was Monet who used white to best effect, sprinkling it throughout his flowerbeds among solid colors to make his flower garden appear as if it were shimmering. He also trained airy white-flowering vines – like white wisteria, *Clematis montana*, and silver fleece vine (*Fallopia*) – high overhead on metal supports so they produced a lace-curtain impression and further added to the shimmering effect of his unique garden.

The post-Impressionist artist, Vincent van Gogh, identified black and orange as a good color harmony for the garden. He noticed that many orange flowers have black centers (for example African daisies, black-eyed Susans and sunflowers). By planting mostly orange-and-black flowers and adding some all-black flowers, such as black irises, black violas and black scabiosa, a dramatic bi-colored combination can be achieved.

1 *Pink garden with nymph statue.* 2 *Formal cool color border, Monet's garden.* 3 *Informal hot color planting, Monet's garden.* 4 *Golden garden, Bellevue garden, New Zealand.* 5 *White garden featuring lupins and arum lilies.*

5   4

Columns, colonnades and pedestals

COLUMNS, COLONNADES AND PEDESTALS are all useful structural accents in the garden, columns supporting pavilions and temple roofs, colonnades utilizing a number of columns aligned like a pergola, and pedestals creating exclamation points at the end of a path, even if they do not support a statue or urn.

Columns and colonnades are for adding a classical or romantic aura to the garden. Near his home, Cezanne cherished a garden attached to a country residence, the Chateau Noir, for its brooding atmosphere. The neo-Gothic house itself was unfinished and made all the more eerie by a row of columns intended to support an orangerie, but never completed. At the end of a terrace, overgrown with ivy, fallen columns lay among old millstones and broken pieces of balustrade. Cezanne valued the place as an inexhaustible source of motifs because of its ruinous state and mystical aura.

Ivy-girdled columns, or columns planted with a rambling rose, clematis or wisteria, will add greatly to the romantic look of a garden. At Winterthur garden, Delaware, a circle of columns provides a meeting space for people to gather and sit on stone seats at a stone circle. Situated in a woodland clearing, it creates an exhedra – a secluded meeting place with origins in Ancient Greek and Roman architecture. This setting is similar to an exhedra in the garden near Paris where Impressionist painter Gustave Caillebotte grew up and painted in his youth. The exhedra on the Caillebotte estate has a semicircle of columns strung with chains along which wisteria vines are trained for added decoration.

1

2

3

4

1 *Indigo columns support terracotta pots, Heronswood garden, Washington State.* 2 *Columned wedding pavilion.* 3 *Colonnade terrace, San Diego.* 4 *Children's fantasy garden, Winterthur, Delaware.*

Composting

COMPOSTING is a good gardening practice, since garden compost can produce superlative plant growth. The popular British garden book, *Encyclopaedia of Gardening* (1850), advised its readers: 'A mixture of stable dung, sea-weed, and vegetable mould, which has lain in a heap for three or four months, and has been two or three times turned during that period, will make an excellent manure for most kinds of garden land. Also, cow-dung, hog-dung, and sheep dung, mixed with soot and with wood ashes.'

Since piles of rotting compost can look unsightly, gardeners today have a wide choice of commercially available bins in which to produce compost. These range from metal bins that can be rotated with a hand crank to turn the compost for fast decomposition, to wooden box-like structures and even special black plastic earthworm bins where the creatures feast on organic waste, pass it through their bodies and expel it as black, fluffy humus rich in plant nutrients.

Essentially, the practice of composting consists of piling garden debris such as grass clippings, hedge trimmings, weeds, spoiled fruit and surplus vegetables, into a pile and allowing it to rot down into a dark, fluffy, organic material called humus that works wonders on impoverished soil. Not only does finished compost improve drainage of compacted clay soil by unbinding clay particles, it improves the moisture-holding capacity of sandy soil, and – properly made – compost adds essential plant nutrients for healthy plant growth. Since compost contains millions of beneficial micro-organisms, the use of compost on abused land – for example, one with a heavy concentration of salts as a result of overuse of commercial fertilizer – can purify the soil, and where trees like black walnuts have poisoned the soil with their roots by the excretion of juglin, the action of micro-organisms in compost will reclaim the soil.

The most attractive compost piles tend to be contained in bins and the size of these will depend on the amount of compost needed. Some bins are circular, made simply from creating a cylinder of wire to hold the waste material, others are square or rectangular structures with slats to provide aeration to the heap. These bins are generally found in pairs: one bin for finished compost and the other for compost in the making.

For the most nutrient-rich compost, add the ingredients in layers, and avoid waste that rots down too slowly like animal fats. Tree branches and large, leathery leaves should be shredded before adding to a compost pile. Start with green material, such as grass clippings and freshly-pulled weeds since these contribute nitrogen which is essential for leafy growth. Then add a layer of wood ashes from fireplaces or burn piles, since wood ashes add potash, essential for overall vigor and disease resistance. A layer of spoiled fruit like banana skins and grapefruit rinds, also bonemeal, will add phosphorus which is responsible for good root development, flowering and fruiting. Animal manures such as stable manure will add more nitrogen. Eggshells can contribute calcium, a trace element, and other trace elements are to be found in shredded leaves. A layer of topsoil will hasten decomposition by adding micro-organisms and earthworms to speed up the process.

For best results add compost to the soil in spring, before planting, and again in autumn after frost and the winter clean-up of beds.

1 *Combination potting bench and compost bin.* 2 *Commercial composter.* 3 *Whimsical compost pile.* 4 *Cylindrical wire compost bin.* 5 *Three-compartment compost bin.*

Conservatories and orangeries

CONSERVATORIES AND ORANGERIES Conservatories are usually glassed-in structures with heat and ample natural light for growing tender plants. They can be freestanding or attached to a house; if the latter, they are sometimes called a sunroom. Most conservatories feature a diverse plant collection, while some concentrate on a special plant family such as ferns, orchids, camellias, bromeliads and even palms.

Popular construction materials for conservatories are rot-resistant redwood, metal (especially long-lasting aluminum) and double-glazed safety glass that provides good insulation and resistance to breakage. Avoid glass-fiber panes and clear plastic as both will discolor with age. Glass admits the clearest light, and even a 1 percent difference in light transmission can mean a 100 percent improvement in flowering; that some-

1 and 2 Conservatory at Rockwood garden, Delaware, exterior and interior views.

1

2

times means the difference between flowers and no flowers. A freestanding conservatory will usually provide better plant growth than a glass-roofed conservatory attached to a residence as a lean-to, since plants prefer all-around light rather than directional light.

In summer, transluscent panes can cause overheating, so some type of shading may be desirable; in which case the shading should be on the outside so the sun's rays are dissipated before they reach the glass.

A small Victorian-style conservatory at Cedaridge Farm is attached to the kitchen and serves as a dining alcove, also a reading room. Though the conservatory features flowering houseplants such as orchids, during winter months it is used to provide cold-weather protection for a fig tree, a lemon and a banana, all of which are placed outdoors during frost-free months, to bear fruit.

Orangeries are buildings of stone or brick with tall arched windows and skylights for the specific purpose of growing citrus fruits in containers. With oranges and other citrus fruits so readily available year round, and inexpensive from grocery stores, orangeries are now little used for growing citrus fruits, and many of them have been converted to sunrooms.

1 *Orangerie at Conestoga House, Pennsylvania.* 2 *Conservatory interior at Cedaridge Farm.* 3 *Lean-to greenhouse, Connecticut garden.* 4 *Conservatory exterior, Cedaridge Farm.*
5 *Conservatory/sunroom at Andalusia, Pennsylvania.*

Containers

CONTAINERS To have attractive container plantings it is not only essential to create visually stimulating color combinations with your live material – it's important to also choose a visually interesting container to complement the plants and their location. When in doubt about what container to use, bear in mind that terracotta pots seem to work well in any location, whether it's a cottage-garden setting or on a contemporary deck. However, one should also consider the sophistication of wooden box-shaped Versailles planters, soy buckets, stone troughs and whiskey half barrels. It's also fun to hunt antique shops and fleamarkets for off-beat containers such as old wicker fish creels, milk cans, chimney flues and peach baskets, even old wheelbarrows and goat carts to hold an assortment of conventional pots. (For window-box ideas

1 *Container grouping with marguerite daisies, foreground.*
2 *Deck planters feature annual vinca, foreground.* 3 *Rustic wheelbarrow planted with primulas.* 4 *Stairway, Cedaridge Farm, featuring assortment of potted annuals.* 5 *Antique cart displays potted herbs.*

1

2

3

5

4

1

2

3

see page 215, and for hanging-basket planters, see page 96.)

When combining plants in containers, strive for several layers of interest. Around the rim, for example, use plants that will spread and drape over the edge like a curtain. The chocolate and chartreuse forms of sweet potato vine (*Ipomoea batatas*) are ideal for this purpose. Above the outer rim, consider a medium-height plant, like compact varieties of coleus. For the third level of interest use a tall plant like a spiky dracaena, yucca or striped canna.

Use as large a container as possible since small containers tend to dry out quickly and may need watering more than once a day. For hot summers, wood, stone and clay are better than plastic or metal, which can overheat quickly and burn tender roots. Remember that certain types of paving can be brutal on plants, reflecting excessive heat and glare to burn leaves. White surfaces in particular, such as white landscape chips and white tilework, should be avoided unless in shade.

Don't use only a commercial potting soil as a growing medium since it can be too light and fluffy to provide good anchorage. Water and nutrients will also tend to drain through it too rapidly. Rather, mix peat-based potting soils with some good garden topsoil. For cacti and succulents, an equal amount of sand or gravel should be added to peat-based potting soils. Good drainage is always essential, so ensure that your containers have a drainage hole. Line the bottom of each pot with a one-inch layer of broken clay crocks, crushed stones or gravel to keep the drainage hole from becoming clogged with compacted soil. To aid drainage even more, consider raising the container above the paving or soil surface

1 *Potted fuchsia in Monet's garden.* 2 *Birdbath functions as a dish planter for sedums.* 3 *Dish planter accents a rock garden.* 4 *Note clay feet used to raise pot above teak table.* 5 *Chard and coleus in window-box planter.* 6 *Strawberry planter.* 7 *Potted succulents on a sunny deck.*

7

4

6

5

with special clay 'feet', bricks or stones. Where the draining away of excess water through the drainage hole will create an unsightly stain (such as on decks and patios), place containers on watering trays.

If you are in the habit of using unconventional containers for growing plants, such as wash tubs, stone troughs, and watering-cans, either drill a hole for drainage, or create a drainage area of loose gravel in the bottom where excess water can collect and drain through evaporation. When watering containers of exotic fruit trees like figs and citrus, avoid using cold water as this can retard growth and fruit yields. Instead, use tepid water.

Fertilizing is essential, and this is best done with a liquid feed applied directly to the root zone, preferably with a long-handled watering wand that is easily poked between stems and leaves to drench the soil. Follow label directions for rates of application, as all brands are not alike. Be aware that many fast-acting fertilizers leave a salty crystal residue in the soil, and this can build up a toxicity. Use new soil every season, and flush the interior walls of pots to leave no salt residue.

It is inadvisable to leave containers outdoors in the winter, even with plants considered to be hardy or evergreen. A raised container can be too susceptible to damage from frost and freezing. If you must leave the container and plant outdoors, bury it up to its rim and over it heap shredded leaves or wood chips for several inches more to protect the plant and pot. Do not leave plantless containers outdoors during winter if they are filled with soil because moisture in the soil may freeze and expand to crack the pot. Rather, empty the soil and turn the container upside down, placing it under shelter.

Container gardening allows people without garden soil to grow plants, for even a wooden stairway, metal catwalk or a tiny concrete backyard can accommodate clusters of containers. Where space is limited, consider growing some edible plants, such as tomatoes and peppers, since these are ever-bearing, or culinary herbs, such as parsley, sage and thyme which are usually needed in relatively small amounts. For generous yields, however, you will need a sunny location. Though there are many flowering plants suitable for shade (impatiens, wishbone flower and tuberous begonias, for example), most herbs and vegetables demand at least eight hours of sunlight for worthwhile yields.

An altogether different form of container gardening is the cultivation of trees and shrubs as bonsai, the Japanese art of dwarfing woody plants. (For information on growing bonsai in special shallow trays, see page 39.)

1 *Pandanus in a glazed blue urn.* 2 *Miniature waterlily in dish planter.* 3 *Potted annuals create a vertical garden.*
4 *Offbeat containers add charm to a patio.*

Courtyards and patios

COURTYARDS AND PATIOS Courtyards are enclosed spaces where stone paving and stone walls produce a pleasant, cool oasis. Sometimes they are located at the entrance to an old residence, providing a place where, before the automobile's advent, visitors were welcomed after dismounting from a carriage. A courtyard can also be a cool, central area open to the elements and designed for relaxation.

In Greek and Roman times a peristyle courtyard was usually rectangular, surrounded by a colonnaded walkway and planted with trees and shrubs in tubs. A peristyle that included a reflecting pool or bathing pool was called a 'veridarium'. A courtyard known as an 'atrium' was often the central room of a Roman villa, open to the sky. Today, an atrium describes a similar open area, but filled with plants, and often with a glass roof to exclude frost. The great advantage of atriums in modern homes is that they are not only sheltered from winds, but also benefit from escaping heat from the house, allowing tender plants like camellias, figs, bananas and tree ferns to be grown in frost-prone areas.

1

3

2

5

4

1 *Cezanne's courtyard, Aix-en-Provence.* 2 *Entrance to Spanish-style courtyard, Casa Pacifica, California.* 3 *Courtyard at Chateau Grimaldi, France.* 4 *Brick patio beside a lake.* 5 *Courtyard of tropical plants.*

Usually, courtyards are shaded by the height of the walls and so shade-loving plants may be more desirable. Courtyards are associated with French and Spanish-style gardens and often feature a fountain as a focal point. The courtyard gardens of New Orleans are world-famous, invariably featuring banana trees in pots to create a tropical aura. Balconies of wrought-iron railings face into the courtyard, and plants in an assortment of containers cascade from the balconies.

A patio is usually an expanse of stone terrace that can be enclosed on three sides, or project out over a slope like a terrace. It serves as an extension of a living space, for outdoor entertaining, and frequently offers a beautiful view.

Both patios and courtyards are good places to feature container plants. They are also suitable for making minimalist designs, using spacious walls as backgrounds for sparse, sculptural plantings.

1 *Courtyard with* Echium wildpretii, *Kerdalo, France.*
2 *Gravel courtyard in Renoir's garden.* 3 *Orange gazanias create a bold contrast with blue courtyard wall.*
4 *Patio planting, Greenwood garden, New Jersey.*

Decks and platforms

DECKS AND PLATFORMS are generally made of rot-resistant wood, like redwood and radiata pine. They are a means of connecting the house interior with the garden exterior, providing a place for outdoor entertaining that is likely to be much less costly than building a porch, veranda or terrace. Though decks and platforms can be freestanding, they allow residents to walk freely from a confined interior to the light and airiness of the great outdoors. Decks are especially popular as extensions of bedrooms to take in a secluded view, and as extensions of dining rooms for the convenience of eating al fresco when the weather is pleasant.

Verandas and porches usually hug the walls of a residence, and are accessible from the front door, while decks and platforms can be built out over a pond or steep slope. The deck pattern can vary, and the wood can be stained or painted to preserve its life. Most local building codes do not allow raised platforms or decks without a railing, and there are regulations regarding width between the struts, to prevent small children from falling through. In spite of these restrictions, the design for a deck can reflect some ingenuity, by its shape (for example semi-circular or octagonal instead of the traditional square and rectangular shape.) Also, a deck can have several levels.

Decks are invaluable where a slope is too steep to cultivate plants. The deck's flat surface then becomes an ideal place to grow plants in pots, perhaps even with a Jacuzzi or hot tub built into the deck.

An especially good site for a deck may be where a mature tree is close to the house. The deck then can either surround the tree, leaving a hole in the middle for it to continue to grow, or the deck can extend under the tree canopy up to the trunk, in both cases providing the benefit of cool shade. For decks exposed to the sun, consider an awning that can be rolled out to cover the deck during inclement weather.

Freestanding decks were first used by the Chinese and Japanese in their gardens as viewing platforms. At the Katsura Imperial Garden, Kyoto, a substantial L-shaped deck juts out over a carp pond to provide a strategic place to view fish swimming below and moon reflections, hence its name, the Moon Viewing Platform.

1

2

3

4

5

1–7 *An assortment of decks and platforms used for difficult-to-plant or confined spaces, including three tiered cantilevered decks over the Pacific Ocean, Big Sur, California.*

7

6

Driveways

DRIVEWAYS can be eyesores, with their large expanses of asphalt or impervious surface, and they are made doubly difficult features to landscape by usually terminating at garage doors which present hideous expanses of wood or metal. Most architects and home builders will take the shortest route from the road to the garage when installing a paved driveway, whereas an attractive gravel surface and a scenic circuitous route might be aesthetically more appealing.

A simple way to landscape a driveway is to plant an avenue of trees to create an allée or leafy tunnel. Driveways can feature wheel tracks instead of asphalt, the wheel tracks paved in Belgium block, or packed gravel, with a median strip of grass or low-growing groundcovers.

There is a tendency to make driveways too long, too short, or too narrow and the parking space too confined, which is understandable since most people would rather devote the space to plantings. Sometimes, the unpretentious location and narrowness of a driveway is deliberate, to give an understated impression for the purpose of discouraging intruders. The best driveways do not terminate in a dead-end so visitors must maneuver their car awkwardly to get back out, but surround a circular feature such as a flowerbed or a clump of low shrubs such as hydrangeas, creating a drive-through entrance and exit. The great New Zealand landscape architect, Alfred Buxton (1872–1950), loved to plant trees to deliberately screen the main residence from the road, and for the house to be revealed at the end of a curving driveway only at the last moment, creating a sense of mystery and anticipation.

1

2   3

1 *Leafy corridor and wheel tracks of Belgium block provide a sense of mystery for a driveway in Britanny.* 2 *Coastal driveway featuring wheel tracks.* 3 *Curved gravel driveway bordered with heather.* 4 *Gravel driveway framed by ivy-girdled tree.*
5 *Lavender softens a straight driveway.* 6 *Asphalt driveway curves across a stone bridge towards the main house.*
7 *Gravel driveway softened by grasses.* 8 *Stone pavers change to gravel at Blake House, California.*

8

4

5

6

7

Dry landscapes

*D*DRY LANDSCAPES The term 'xeriscape' describes the conservation of water through creative landscaping, derived from the Greek 'xeros' meaning dry, and 'scape', which infers a particular habitat or setting. Though mostly associated with desert landscapes and sparse rainfall, the idea of conserving water is important even in regions with relatively high rainfall because rain doesn't always come when it is needed, especially during summer months.

Water conservation does not necessarily mean the avoidance of water features. Indeed a water feature is almost always incorporated into dry landscapes for the refreshing visual sight it produces, but the water is recirculated so it is not wasted, and the evaporation area is reduced in size to a small running stream, or merely a water basin for birds to drink at and bathe. Efficient irrigation is also a part of good xeriscaping, since water applied directly to the root zone by covered drip lines, for example, is much less wasteful of precious water than overhead sprinklers which deluge paths and other hardscape areas. Similarly, the application of mulches will greatly reduce water evaporation from soil, aid in moisture penetration, reduce weed competition for water, moderate soil temperature to reduce heat loss, control soil erosion, and provide a decorative alternative to bare or stony soil.

Above all, xeriscaping is about sensible plant selection, and these choices will vary from region to region, depending mostly on the likelihood and degree of frost. Many hardy plants, such as shrub hibiscus (*Hibiscus syriacus*), butterfly bushes (*Buddleja*) and butterfly weed (*Asclepias*), require supplemental watering only to get established. Cacti and succulents are the principal components of dry landscapes in frost-free areas because they are mostly frost tender, although there is a hardy prickly-pear cactus (*Opuntia humifusa*), plus many kinds of hardy euphorbia, sedums and yucca that make good substitutes for cacti.

Typically, cacti are barrel-shaped to store water during dry spells, and they are covered with sharp spines to protect themselves from foraging animals. They generally lack leaves to reduce moisture loss, thriving in open, sunny locations where

1

7

6

1 *Succulent collection, Bellevue garden, New Zealand.* 2 *Coastal garden, New Zealand.* 3 *Desert garden at Huntington Botanical Garden, California.*
4 *Variegated agave at Marjorelle garden, Morocco.* 5 *Dry landscape featuring drifts of grey lavender cotton.*
6 *Small-space planting of lythops.*
7 *Dry landscape at Tresco Abbey gardens, UK.*

little else is capable of growing. Surprisingly, cacti have some of the most beautiful flowers in the plant kingdom and they make good collections for growing in conservatories.

Because cacti and succulents can look stiff and bizarre in landscape plantings, it's good to include some drought-tolerant perennials such as English lavender, Siberian sage and ornamental grasses, especially varieties of maiden grass (*Miscanthus*) and fountain grass (*Pennisetum*), for the contrast their slender, arching leaf blades can provide.

Sedums of all kinds have succulent leaves with a plant habit that can be low and ground-hugging (for example, *Sedum spurium* 'Dragon's Blood'), to upright and bushy like the pink-flowering 'Brilliant' and rusty-red 'Autumn Joy', variations of *Sedum spectabile*.

One of the world's most unusual dry landscapes is at the Huntington Botanical Garden, San Marino, California, where wealthy industrialist Henry Huntington established an Italianate home and a series of spacious theme gardens around the imposing residence. Started in 1903 with the purchase of

a cattle ranch, the gardens were opened to the public in 1927. Huntington's head gardener, William Hertrich, had a passion for cacti and succulents at a time when they were thought to be bizarre, prickly nuisance plants, of little value for embellishing a garden. However, Hertrich collected together some 4000 species to establish a Desert Garden. Twelve acres in extent, it is now the main garden attraction at Huntington. Similar dry landscape gardens exist in Europe along the Mediterranean coast, for example the 'jardins exotiques' at Eze (France), Monaco, and Bordighera (Italy). All three are laid out along trails that hug the sides of precipitous cliffs, on the same stretch of coast.

In Great Britain, Tresco Abbey Gardens, in the Isles of Scilly, have impressive dry landscapes, but on a more modest scale the gravel garden of British horticulturist Beth Chatto is an inspirational example. A theme garden that is never watered, and was once a parched parking lot, her dry landscape has become the subject of a colorful book, *Beth Chatto's Gravel Garden* (Frances Lincoln, 2000).

Edging

EDGING is important beside paths and lawns and wherever there is a sudden change from hardscape to softscape. The type of edging to use can be determined by the theme of the garden. Loops of bamboo are popular in Oriental gardens, bricks laid on end, tilted to create a saw-tooth design, feature in American colonial gardens, wicker suits vegetable and herb gardens and smooth, rounded, sugarloaf-shaped boulders can edge a path or flowerbed in a coastal garden.

Edgings can also be composed of low, spreading plants. To edge the sunny beds of his Clos Normand flower garden, Claude Monet favored aubrieta. In shady areas at Cedaridge Farm, clump-forming liriope is used.

Where a lawn and flowerbed meet, it is best to consider an edging that lies flat, recessed to just below the cutting height of the grass so mower blades can make a clean, not eroded, edge to the lawn and not cut into the plantings.

Garden centers stock many kinds of lawn edging, including rubber and aluminum strips that can uncoil to make a straight edge between turf and soil, but these can look ugly and they are not nearly as attractive as a ribbon of sunken bricks laid edge to edge. For maximum economy an organic mulch such as shredded pine bark can be laid between the lawn and plantings to a height that is almost flush with the cutting height of the grass. Although wood chips and gravel will be scattered by mower blades, shredded pine bark will pack down to stay in place.

1 Low bamboo edging. 2 Brick edging in a Charleston, South Carolina, garden. 3 Low wattle fencing in a vegetable garden. 4 Aubrieta edging Monet's gravel paths.

1

2

4

3

English cottage gardens

ENGLISH COTTAGE GARDENS English gardens today conjure up visions of an exuberance of flowers, a sort of organized chaos. This is the antithesis of an Italian garden, for example, which conjures up visions of hardscape – terraces, steps, fountains and statues on pedestals; or a French garden with its vistas leading off into infinity, and elaborate parterres resembling embroidery; or an Islamic garden with its strict geometry of water channels overlooked by a pavilion of intricate stone fretwork. Though the 200 years between 1680 and 1880 produced great garden landscapes in England, inspired by Italian, French and Islamic garden design, it is the cottage garden at which the British excel – a revolt, in fact, against the largesse, geometry (and sometimes vulgarity) of the formal landscape garden.

Significantly, the revolt in British gardening occurred during the Victorian era as a reaction against rigid carpet bedding. The catalyst was an Irishman, William Robinson, a prolific writer who took charge of the herbaceous borders of the Royal Botanic Society in Regent's Park, London. He was fond of English wildflowers and also of cottage gardens he discovered in the countryside. The purpose of his popular book, *The English Flower Garden* (1883) was 'To uproot the idea that a flower garden must always be a set pattern on one side of the house.' His preference was to create a wild garden using 'plants from other countries as hardy as our hardiest wildflowers…as if they were wild flowers, without further cost or care.'

1

2

5

4

3

1 *Cottage garden with lupins, Scotland.* **2** *Welsh cottage cloaked in evergreen euonymus.* **3** *Cottage garden with rustic gate.* **4** *Climbing roses frame a cottage entrance.* **5** *Historic pioneer cottage, Christchurch, New Zealand.*

Robinson's main target was Sir Joseph Paxton's elaborate patterned garden at The Crystal Palace, made in 1854. This ostentation, in Robinson's opinion, was 'The fruit of a poor ambition to outdo another ugly extravagance – Versailles.' He spoke out against the rigid formality of wall and stone, fountains and sculpture, and preferred to see shrubs and trees planted naturalistically to follow the contours of the existing property. He published a magazine, *Gardening Illustrated*, to further his cause and enlisted the support of the great Victorian plantsperson, Gertrude Jekyll, as a frequent contributor of both writing and photography.

In France, a similar concept to the English cottage garden is called the 'Clos Normand', in deference to the quaint cottage gardens of Normandy. In both countries such gardens rely heavily on plants, especially perennials and roses, to present an abundance of color. Structural elements are usually sparse – a walled enclosure of rough stone fleeced with vines, an ornate metal or rustic wooden gate, an unobtrusive sundial, perhaps a rustic arbor, a small dovecote or lattice gazebo threaded with clematis. If an actual thatched guest cottage can feature in the background, and if fragrant flowering plants like lavender and pinks can pervade the air with pleasant aromas, so much the better.

Certain plant species are synonymous with English cottage gardens. They tend to be spire-like plants such as foxgloves, lupins, hollyhocks and delphiniums. Climbing roses or shrub roses are preferred over highly bred hybrid teas and floribundas, and cushion-shaped plants are conspicuous as edging, for example aubrieta, armeria, Serbian bellflower and cheddar pinks. Perennial plants to attract butterflies are also important, such as butterfly bush (*Buddleja*), scarlet lobelia, butterfly weed (*Asclepias tuberosa*), and everblooming old-fashioned annuals such as nasturtium, French marigolds and love-in-a-mist. Though paths can be straight in an English cottage garden, the plantings must be highly informal, with plants encouraged to spill on to walkways and over steps.

1 *Climbing roses help extend color above eye level.*
2 *Welsh cottage covered in Virginia creeper.* 3 *Sunflower and calliopsis enliven a small cottage garden.* 4 *Cottage garden at Cedaridge Farm.*

Entrances

ENTRANCES to residences are the first impression a visitor will form and so they should not only reflect the style of house or personality of the owners, they should say welcome. Entrances to gardens should also create a good first impression, hint at the style of garden, and again make visitors feel welcome, unless the intention is to evoke a surprise or sinister feeling.

In addition to the door itself, the entrance to a residence can feature a number of embellishments: steps leading up to it, a pair of sentinels such as sphinxes, a lintel over the door, an ornate doorbell, an ornate door lock, even a moat in the case of some historic houses.

'If it is not obvious where to park, if there is no parking space, if you stumble in the dark looking for the front door, or mistake the kitchen door for the entrance, these are annoyances that do not say welcome,' wrote Frank Church. He also noted that a small house will appear larger and more dignified when it is saved from the obscurity of heavy tree and shrub plantings. He advised that trees and shrubs along the house foundation can obscure views from windows, reduce light to the house interior, make a residence look old, gloomy and decrepit, and seem suffocating.

For a garden entrance it is generally sufficient to feature a distinctive gate or arbor, remembering that a gate visitors can see through will be more welcoming than a solid gate, which by its opaqueness will say 'private, keep out'. For added appeal, a garden entrance can feature sentinels, particularly plant sentinels like conical Alberta spruce, or an inviting archway.

1 *Red roses echo red front door.* 2 *Imposing entrance to a woodland garden.* 3 *Rustic entrance to a guest cottage.*
4 *Brick arch with metal grill gate says 'welcome'.*

1

4

3

2

Espalier

1

ESPALIER is the practice of training trees and shrubs flat against a wall or trellis. The word is derived from the Italian *spalla*, meaning 'shoulder'. Though many kinds of woody plants with pliable branches can be espaliered – such as evergreen grandiflora magnolias to perfectly display their huge fragrant flowers, and firethorn to display its berry-laden branches – it is fruit trees that are most commonly grown this way. It is not only decorative to see fruit-tree limbs splayed out in a pattern, their branches studded with ripening fruit, but it is also space-saving, allowing maximum yields in minimum space. Fruit trees that respond well to being espaliered include apple, pear, peach, plum, fig, grape and kiwi.

When training any plant against a wall, however, be sure the wall receives full sun, although pears will tolerate some shade. Also, avoid whitewashed walls, as the reflective surface can be too hot in summer, causing sunscald and fostering disease. Training the trees can create interesting patterns – diamond shapes, for example, and even hearts.

One of the finest fruit gardens anywhere can be seen at Eleutherian Mills, Delaware, where Eleuthere Irenee duPont – founder of the duPont chemical dynasty – established his house and garden in the French style, with an emphasis on espaliered fruit trees. Apple trees, for example, are trained over an arbor to form a tunnel, and as 'cordons' (ropes) along low fence rails to form an edging to paths. Pear trees are trained into compact cone shapes or spindles. Peaches have their branches splayed out like a fan on a free-standing trellis of wooden slats, and woven into each other to create a living fence.

Today, cordons of apple trees are used as low 'living fences' at the edge of lawns in Monet's garden, where spires of pear trees are also trained flat against a wall.

2

4

1 *Fruit trees espaliered on a cottage.*
2 *Apple cordons in Monet's garden.* 3
Apple espalier trained to make a heart shape. 4 *Firethorn espalier.*

3

Evening gardens

EVENING GARDENS are gardens designed to look good by the light of the moon. This necessitates a lot of pale-colored flowers, especially white, cream, pale yellow and pale pink. Evening gardens are also enhanced by the presence of fragrant plants, since many of these release their exotic scents only in the late afternoon or evening, in order to attract moths and bats as pollinators. This includes night-scented stock, moonflowers, night-blooming cereus, old-fashioned sweet peas, jasmine, night-blooming waterlilies, and the strawberry shrub (*Calycanthus floridus*).

A garden for evening pleasure can also feature white structures such as marble or limestone balustrades, and a white gazebo. At Cedaridge Farm, a white arch is positioned where the moon rises above the horizon during summer, so the arch will frame the moon as it climbs up into the sky. The foreground is planted with mostly white shrub roses, and white annuals, including alyssum, petunias, larkspur and snapdragons.

A small water basin or small pool is also a good idea in order to catch the moon's reflection. Pools and ponds can feature a fragrant white waterlily.

1

4

1 Moon garden with white arch, Cedaridge Farm. 2 White datura at twilight, Cedaridge Farm. 3 White marguerite daisies and delphiniums echo white Spanish-style residence. 4 White gazebo and bird box echo white plantings.

3

2

Fences

FENCES The first advice in a medieval book on gardening is to 'Fence in your garden'. Since the book was written at a time of hardship and poverty, thievery was common and so a fence was considered essential. Even today, where a garden may feature a vegetable plot or flowers for cutting, fencing is an economical way to ensure privacy and security from unwanted intruders, and also to keep out foraging animals such as rabbits and deer.

'The gateway to the American colonial garden was through the post-and-rail fence,' wrote Dr. William M. Klein Jr. in *Gardens of Philadelphia and the Delaware Valley* (1995). According to Klein, these rustic fences were not intended for security or even to keep animals out of a pioneer property, since intruders could easily crawl through it and deer jump over it, 'but to hold back the monumental green wall of the Eastern deciduous forest. Within these fences, the colonial farms and gardens were the life-support systems that carried European agriculture and gardening traditions to the New World.'

Certainly, easily-erected split-rail fences in colonial America marked a line that the wilderness was not supposed to cross, but nowhere in the world is the art of building a security fence more refined than in the ancient city of Kyoto, Japan. Many properties use bamboo fences aligned shoulder-to-shoulder to present a solid barrier, others feature the bamboo widely spaced like trelliswork, in order to see through it. Some fences combine both styles, a solid barrier at the bottom and a see-through design at the top. Bamboo is a wonderful renewable resource to use for fencing because it looks natural, and it is available in several distinct colors including yellow, blue and black in addition to green. Thickness of bamboo can vary considerably from severe-looking, solid, pole-like canes making the most solid barriers, to more refined, friendlier-looking thin, spindly canes that can still make impenetrable barriers when bunched together for a matted screen.

Another good city to view decorative fence styles is the historic district of Colonial Williamsburg, Virginia. Though the fences are restorations of styles used by American colonists, mostly from Great Britain, they present a wide range of designs, from rustic 'worm' fences used as boundaries for farmsteads, to elaborate wrought-iron metal fences bordering the more substantial town houses of professional people like doctors and lawyers.

When choosing a fence, consider if you want to be able to look through it or step over it, or whether you want it to be a solid barrier. Mostly made from wood, fencing can be much less expensive than building a stone wall, and it is quicker to install and needs much less maintenance than trying to grow a healthy barrier hedge, though even the most decorative fencing is rarely as attractive as a dense, uniform hedge.

Particular styles of fence are associated with special parts of the country. Black cast-iron fences with an ornate cornstalk motif are popular in American colonial cities such as New

1

6   5

1 *Deer fence in a suburban garden, Connecticut.* 2 *Modernistic screening fence made from wooden blocks, Garrett Eckbo garden, California.* 3 *American colonial-style picket fence.* 4 *Woven bamboo screening fence.* 5 *Oriental-style fence.* 6 *Paling fence threaded with roses.*

Orleans and Charleston. Wooden paling fences made from rough redwood grape stakes feature prominently in the resort town of Carmel, California, while white wooden Chinese lattice patterns are common in Colonial Williamsburg. Rural areas of England favor wattle fences, and driftwood and

2

4

3

metal farm wheels often decorate fences in rural areas of Australia and New Zealand. Cedaridge Farm has a white ranch-style fence surrounding the property. (See page 84.) The main gate is a similar design with a criss-cross pattern of wooden boards, which was featured in a famous painting by the Impressionist painter, Gustave Caillebotte, of his garden near Paris.

The most popular style of fence for cottages and residential houses is the traditional white picket fence that extends to chest height and allows people to view over it. Precut styles are available from lumber suppliers. They are quick to install and allow plants like rambler roses and morning glories to thread their stems through gaps between the pickets.

Panel, paling or stockade fences provide more privacy than picket fences, since they generally extend above head height and the wooden uprights butt together to block any view on the other side. Mostly made of wood, they can look ugly unless the monotonous expanse is decorated with a vine. Consider planting climbing roses, clematis vines, honeysuckle and even annual morning glories against the fence, training their stems to nails for support. Lattice fences have the benefit of allowing people to see through them, and for vining plants to thread their stems through unaided. Wooden rail fences can look good in rural locations, especially where a division is needed between a garden and a meadow or woodland. They are especially good to use as a barrier against livestock such as sheep and cattle wandering into a property. For extra embellishment, rambling roses, clematis and trumpet creeper can be trained along the rails.

Wattle fences are mostly made from willow branches (called withies) or bamboo, since they are both durable and flexible enough to weave between closely-spaced stakes to create a solid barrier. They are more attractive than paling fences, and they are good to consider if you want a low fence to step over, such as an edging to a flower border or a divider in an herb garden.

For longevity, fence posts should be set into concrete that extends below the frost line to prevent 'heaving.' Using a post-hole digger, excavate a round hole double the diameter of the fence post. The bottom should be filled with gravel to aid drainage and a stable base on which to pour the concrete.

Every fence needs a gate, and though gates most often match the style of fence (a bamboo gate for a bamboo fence), this is not always the case. A gate can be much more decorative than the fence. (See pages 84–5.)

When descending a slope, consider whether you want the fence to step down in a series of flat, horizontal sections, or whether you want the fence line to follow the contour of the slope. Generally speaking, a fence that steps down in equal level spans looks better. Also, decide whether you want your fence to run in a straight line or whether it might look more attractive if it snaked across the landscape. Straight lines can look austere, as opposed to meandering lines that can look less contrived.

1

1 *Wrought-iron fence garlanded with sweet autumn clematis.* 2 *Stepped picket fence.* 3 *Worm fence.* 4 *Fence of sheep hurdles.* 5 *Picket fence with wavy top.* 6 *Baton fence softened with climbing roses.* 7 *See-through wattle fence and mister.* 8 *Wattle screening fence.* 9 *Ornate fence, Colonial Williamsburg, Virginia.* 10 *Vine-covered wrought-iron fence, Hotel Baudy, Giverny, France.*

10

2

3

9

4

5

6

8

7

Fern gardens

FERN GARDENS can be wonderful quiet, eerie places to discover in a woodland garden, or in the shade of a building. Also, since many exotic ferns (like stag's horn and tree ferns) are tender to frost, they often occupy a special niche in a conservatory. Outdoors, they are most often associated with grottoes and woodland, where a moist atmosphere can encourage the healthiest and most diverse fern growth. It is hardly surprising that one of the world's largest outdoor fern gardens, the Fernz Fern Garden, is in Auckland, New Zealand, since many ferns are indigenous to New Zealand's North and South islands, particularly Fiordland National Park.

At the Morris Arboretum, near Philadelphia, a Victorian-style conservatory is devoted to ferns, including both hardy maidenhair ferns and tropical tree ferns. The ferns are displayed among boulders along a path that encircles a pool at the bottom of a ravine. It crosses a rustic wooden bridge, enters a grotto with steps leading down and up the other side, and passes under a stone arch. Steps leading out of the stone arch then climb to an observation platform for a high-elevation view of the entire fern collection.

1

6

5

2

4

1 *Fernz Fern Garden, Auckland.* **2** *Roadside ferns, Fiordland National Park, New Zealand.* **3** *Morris Fernery, Pennsylvania.* **4** *Ferns and grasses, Heligan garden, UK.* **5** *Fern-fringed pool.* **6** *Rhododendron and ostrich ferns.*

3

Fountains

FOUNTAINS are useful devices to suddenly introduce water into a garden space, though as decorative accents they offend a lot of garden purists because they are more often a tribute to modern technology than anything to do with nature. Monet was one of these purists who disliked fountains. Except for geysers and coastal blowholes that provide brief plumes of spray in naturalistic surroundings, nature does not produce the vertical crescendos of spray often associated with the most ostentatious fountains, such as those at Versailles Palace, near Paris, and the Villa d'Este, near Rome. When fountains are too elaborate there is often the thought that hidden underground is an intricate system of plumbing and pumps humming away and waiting to break down.

Fountain styles for gardens vary according to whether the garden is formal or informal, from traditional to contemporary, mostly using metal or stone, since water can quickly rot wood. Myriad variations are possible with the jets of water, not only with regard to height and angle of play but also by

1

3

2

1 *Small bubbling fountain, Keukenhof, Holland.* **2** *Avenue of 100 fountains, Villa d'Este, Italy.* **3** *Rock pool decorated with small, unpretentious frothing fountain.*

1

1 *Fountain at Holker Hall, UK.* 2 *Wall fountain detail, Chanticleer garden, USA.* 3 *Informal pool with slender water jet.*

various forms of movement, such as swirling and spiraling, arching and dancing, even computerized to correspond to crescendos of sound from piped music. As gravity pulls the spuming water back to earth, all manner of catchments can be incorporated, such as raised pools and clusters of boulders to produce clouds of fine spray. And of course, fountains can be lit imaginatively for even more dramatic effect, a range of spotlights timed to create a veritable fireworks display of colored spray.

The Romans were fond of bathing in special bath-houses and they adored fountains. In fact, a book written in the first century AD, *De Aquis Urbis Romae*, by a Roman Supervisor of Water Supply, Sextus Julius Frontinus, gave instructions for the construction of water features, including the plumbing needed to create fountains. The word fountain comes from the Latin *fons*, meaning a spring, and in Roman and Ancient Greek times a fountain was invariably the predominant ornamental accent for a courtyard. Usually this would be bowl-shaped, with the water rising in a jet from the middle, or spewing from faces set into stone walls, gushing, dribbling or jetting out in an arc from the mouth of a maiden, cupid or devil face. Fountains in these ancient gardens invariably dripped over the edges of a catchment basin at the base, to feed channels that led to formal pools or irrigated parts of the enclosed garden.

2

3

Framing

FRAMING is one of the most important design features for a well-designed garden, whether formal or informal, because framing helps to give the garden a sense of depth and perspective, and in small gardens creates the illusion of greater distance. Just as artists must decide the appropriate frame for a painting to make it stand out, so gardens need framing elements to isolate design details and views. Frequently the framing can be accomplished with tree branches arching their limbs over a scene. This is particularly important with a breathtaking panoramic view because the view will widen out to its full extent when a visitor steps through the shadowy frame, and produce two visual sensations: a framed view and an unframed one. At other times the framing can be done with a structure, such as a moongate or an archway.

Other design devices that produce a frame are leafy tunnels such as avenues and pleached alleys, covered gateways and bridges, covered porches and verandas, picture windows and arching water jets. Claude Monet's garden features numerous framing elements. In his Clos Normand flower garden there is the Grande Allée, a floral tunnel that frames the house entrance from the bottom of the garden, while in the water garden rose arches over the boat dock frame his waterlilies and the pond's reflections.

1

5

4

3

1 Live oak frames main residence, Magnolia Plantation, South Carolina. 2 Cherry blossoms frame a grass path. 3 Hedge and trees frame a thatched cottage. 4 Japanese gateway frames a moss garden. 5 Rose arches in Monet's garden.

French gardens

FRENCH GARDENS historically are symbols of wealth and power. From the 1600s to the late nineteenth century they took inspiration mostly from highly formal Italian gardens like the Villa d'Este, near Rome. Vaux-le-Vicomte, south of Paris, echoes the perfection and symmetry of the Villa d'Este, but on a flat plane, rather than a steep slope. Built by Nicolas Fouquet in 1650, Vaux-le-Vicomte set a new standard for ostentatious design in French gardens. Requiring 18,000 workers to construct, the chateau and its vast garden were conceived as a property to impress important people, for Fouquet was the Sun King's minister of finance. But when Louis XIV saw how his subject had eclipsed the young king's own stature, he had Fouquet thrown in prison, where he died 19 years later.

The king meanwhile hired Fouquet's design team to build what became the ultimate symbol of wealth and power, the palace and gardens of Versailles. Out of a vast swampland, Fouquet's landscape architect, André Le Nôtre, created a garden of unbelievable size, with a main central axis that extends more than three-quarters of a mile, incorporating a canal for pleasure boating. Pleached alleys, elaborate parterres, hundreds of statues, magnificent fountains, a huge sunken garden, an orangerie for the growing of citrus, a menagerie, and an extensive potager garden, were all incorporated into the overall plan. In later years Versailles was imitated by wealthy people in many parts of the world, including the USA where copies of Versailles became a status symbol, and many of these gardens are now tourist destinations, like Nemours in Delaware; Old Westbury on Long Island; and Biltmore Estate, near Asheville, North Carolina.

Less than thirty minutes drive from Versailles, in the village of Giverny, on the River Seine, is a much less ostentatious French garden that many consider has influenced garden design worldwide even more than Vaux-le-Vicomte and Versailles. It is the creation of the French Impressionist painter Claude Monet, whose restored property of only five acres is now one of the most-visited garden destinations in Europe.

It was in 1980 that a million-dollar donation from Lila Acheson Wallace, publisher of *Readers' Digest* magazine, helped restore Monet's garden. Though Monet wrote little about his garden philosophy, except to say he considered it his

1

greatest work of art, a number of eye-witness accounts written by journalists have allowed the present administration, the Académie des Beaux-Arts, to recreate Monet's favorite color themes, and also the shimmering sensation he achieved by planting lots of airy white flowers.

Other trend-setting gardens of the Impressionists that have been restored are Cezanne's Les Lauves, a woodland garden at Aix-en-Provence, and Renoir's Les Collettes, an ancient olive tree orchard at Cagnes-sur-Mer, near Nice.

In keeping with its reputation for good food, France is also famous for its potager (or kitchen) gardens, none more beautiful than at Villandry, near Tours, where a spacious square parterre garden that uses vegetables for carpet bedding, fruit trees for vertical accents and herbs for edging, covers around 2 ½ acres.

A term often used to describe a French garden is 'rococo', derived from the French *rocaille*, meaning 'rockwork' and also 'fanciful designs of pebbles and shells'. Rococo gardens strike a note of gaiety, using lighthearted, playful and romantic ornamentation such as a grotto, swing seats, an elegant gazebo and a maze.

7　　　6

1 *Villa Ile de France, near Nice.*
2 *Fountain, Vaux-le-Vicomte, near Paris.*
3 *Parterres at Villandry, near Tours.*
4 *Gazebo and canal at Versailles Palace.*
5 *Venus Victorious statue, Renoir's garden, Cagnes-sur-Mer.* 6 *Cherub sculpture, Château de Canon, near Caen.* 7 *Bench in Monet's garden.*

Gates

GATES are mostly used as entrances to gardens and generally the intention is to make a good first impression, though in some cases they need to deter unwanted intruders from entering a garden space. Since gates can be the first design element a visitor sees when entering a garden space, the style of gate should make a statement, whether friendly or uninviting, and make a person curious about the garden beyond.

Gates can help entrances look inviting by being low or composed of slats, allowing people to see beyond, or they can be opaque, a wooden or metal barrier blocking out the interior. Renoir's garden has wrought-iron gates visitors can see through, matching the iron railing fence that surrounds the property. Cezanne's garden has a carriage door set into a high stone wall, its appearance saying 'Keep Out!' Monet's garden has four entrances, and all the gates are opaque and painted green to match the shutters of the main house. He did not want people entering without his permission, and wanted no one painting his garden other than himself.

Ornate gates with wooden slats or metal grillwork (or combinations of the two) can arouse curiosity, especially if left ajar. Solid gates can also act like a theater curtain, to dramatically reveal some sensational view or feature, like a sunken garden or an exhilarating view of the sea. A gate can be deceptive. Deliberately it can be unobtrusive, fooling people into believing nothing of much consequence lies behind it, or it can be highly ostentatious, speaking of wealth and indicating that something grand and visually exciting lies beyond.

Generally the gate will reflect the style of fencing, (for example bamboo) or echo a wall (a gothic or arched shape for a fieldstone enclosure), but more often than not a gate will reflect the style of garden that is beyond the enclosure – perhaps a Chinese-style lych gate to announce a Chinese garden, for example. Such roofed gates are popular in Oriental gardens, and are often thatched or tiled, as places to wait for a guide. In Europe they were once used exclusively for churchyards, the wide overhanging eaves providing shelter for pallbearers while the burial service was read, but in recent years they have become popular for entrances to estate gardens. Though many of these European lych gates are thatched like the Orientals, slate and wooden shakes are now more common.

Gates may not need roofs, but they do need pillars, one to hang hinges and the other so the gate can be latched. Hinges and latches both can be decorative. Pillars can be unobtrusive so nothing detracts from the pattern of the gate itself, or they can be substantial, an integral part of the gate design – for example, tall brick or stone pillars for framing a wrought-iron gate, perhaps with a pair of pineapple finials like so many entrances to Scottish castles or French chateaux.

At Colonial Williamsburg, Virginia, there are a number of picket gates popular during the colonizing of America. They feature a chain with a cannonball slung beneath, so after the gate has been opened , it closes automatically from the weight of the cannonball.

1

7

1 *Arched gateway, cottage garden.*
2 *American colonial-style picket gate and ranch fence.* 3 *Cannonball and chain used as automatic gate closer, Colonial Williamsburg, USA.* 4 *Japanese-style entrance gate.* 5 *Picket gate between hydrangeas.* 6 *Wrought-iron gate at entrance to a secret garden.*
7 *Entrance gate to Cedaridge Farm.*

Gazebos and belvederes

GAZEBOS AND BELVEDERES are decorative shelters generally made of wood, stone or wire for the purpose of taking in a view. Belvederes are similar to gazebos, but usually these are connected to a structure, such as a stone wall, or elevated high off the ground to provide a bird's-eye view. The term gazebo is supposedly derived from 'gaze about', though in modern gardens a gazebo is just as likely to be tucked away in a secluded place as a shelter for reading and contemplation. There are many styles, including Oriental, though Victorian is extremely popular, especially in gardens where wedding ceremonies are conducted. Victorian gazebos feature ornate latticework and gingerbread trim, and are mostly painted white to stand out prominently in the landscape. Victorian-style gazebos are so popular they can be ordered through the mail as a kit and erected as a do-it-yourself project.

Popular places for gazebos are beside a lake, atop a hill, at the start of a vista and in front of an especially attractive scenic feature such as a waterfall. Gazebos are usually open to the environment and in plan view are often circular or octagonal. If furnished, they may feature a built-in wrap-around bench facing the entrance, and sometimes a table for reading or placing a floral arrangement.

The placement of a gazebo as a lookout is vital, not only to ensure the best view but to make a visually interesting focal point at the end of a path or avenue. Gazebos are often painted a color that echoes plants in the vicinity, such as a colony of all-white flowers. The color can also echo other structures in the vicinity, such as a red bridge or green arbor. At the Ladew Topiary Gardens in Maryland, an Oriental-style gazebo is painted black and orange to complement the colors in an orange-and-yellow garden and Japanese maples with charcoal-gray trunks.

There is tremendous scope for originality of design, and distinctive gazebos can often help to readily identify an ethnic theme, such as Japanese or Italian, and even serve as a garden's trademark. For example, the private garden of florist Renny Reynolds at his home in the Pennsylvania countryside features a unique design of white gazebo with sleek lines and a rakish slatted roof like a church spire. The structure stands out over a pond, connected to the shoreline by a boardwalk, and in photographs is unmistakable as 'Renny's gazebo'.

Cedaridge Farm has a distinctive Victorian-style gazebo with gingerbread trim that has been published in dozens of calendars. It is positioned mid-way up a slope on a level section with a cutting garden in front of it. In such a prominent position it acts as a point of reference for exploring the garden. Though the gazebo remains static the plantings in front of it change with the seasons. In spring the gazebo garden is usually filled with tulips, followed by flowering annuals during summer, and generally cushion chrysanthemums for autumn. One summer season it featured an all-blue theme, and another year the foreground was filled with poppies to create a miniature wildflower meadow. The gazebo garden is

1

2   3

7

4

5

6

1 *Japanese teahouse and belvedere.*
2 Stone belvedere. 3 Vine-covered gazebo
facing herb garden. 4 Rustic woodland
gazebo. 5 Gazebo with dovecote on top.
6 Gazebo built over lake. 7 Victorian-
style wire gazebo.

defined by low boxwood and Japanese yew hedges, with an ornate gate providing entrance along a flagstone path. Behind the gazebo are a mature sugar maple and an ancient English walnut, and in winter when the garden is cloaked in snow it is like a Christmas-card scene – truly a garden for all seasons.

Though gazebos may need no embellishment to look attractive, they are frequently good places to consider covering with vines, if not completely then partially. This can evoke a more romantic atmosphere, especially if the vines bear fragrant flowers like honeysuckle and jasmine. Other good vines to consider for gazebo decoration are climbing roses, silver fleece vine, trumpet creeper and clematis.

Belvedere towers serve the same purpose as a gazebo – to provide a splendid view. Some look like castle turrets, others resemble Chinese pagodas, like the 10-storey pagoda at Kew Gardens, England. Windmills and water towers disguised as fortifications not only serve the practical purpose of pumping water – catwalks around the top turn the structure into a belvedere. In coastal areas, like Mendocino, California, and Mystic Seaport, Connecticut, whale-watch towers – once used to spot whales far at sea – can also serve as belvederes, freestanding on a promontory or attached to a building.

Gazebos can be made more elaborate to serve as more than an outdoor shelter. Japanese teahouses – simple bamboo structures in which were conducted Japanese tea ceremonies – can do double duty as gazebos. Similarly, different kinds of 'temples' need no longer be associated with religious ceremonies but serve as a classical style of gazebo. By glassing in the sides, a gazebo can become a summerhouse or a pavilion to contain a writing desk and a library.

The term 'kiosk' is sometimes used to describe a gazebo. A derivative of the French word, *kiosque*, the term is used to describe a bandstand and also a particular type of ornate garden shelter that is usually slender in construction, with clean lines and a bulbous or peaked roof. The French word is from the Turkish, *koshk*, meaning a pavilion. Kiosks, therefore, are generally gazebos that reflect their exotic Middle-eastern origins, often with mosque-like roofs and windows.

1

6

7

1 *Belvedere on stilts, Trotts Garden, New Zealand.*
2 *Belvedere, Larnach Castle, New Zealand.* 3 *Ivy-covered gazebo.* 4 *Thatched gazebo, Garden House, UK.* 5 *Rustic belvedere, Titoki Point garden, New Zealand.* 6 *Two-storey belvedere surrounded by chess pieces.* 7 *Temple-like gazebo with white 'Climbing Iceberg' roses.*

2

3

4

5

Gazing balls and concretions

GAZING BALLS AND CONCRETIONS Gazing balls can look out of place in gardens, and are regarded with the same disdain afforded gnomes and plastic pink flamingoes by garden purists. However, even sophisticated gardens will sometimes feature gazing balls on pedestals as a focal point, including the famous Butchard Gardens, Vancouver Island, which has a bright, shiny, metallic gazing ball at the center of its formal rose garden.

Balls that are not reflective, but offer an interesting tactile surface or visually interesting texture, are good alternatives to shiny gazing balls. For example, concretions formed by volcanic activity are perfectly round concrete-like boulders that many people like to place on pedestals, group in a pile to form a pyramid, or randomly scatter about the garden like dinosaur eggs. In seaside areas of New Zealand, such as Gore Bay, in the South Island, soil erosion along the shoreline continues to expose such concretions, which have become so popular as outdoor ornaments with the local inhabitants, that they are now a coastal garden trademark for the area.

1 *Pyramid of concretions and sedum.* 2 *Concretions and orchids.* 3 *Marble sphere decorative accent.* 4 *Shiny gazing ball, Butchard Gardens, Canada.* 5 *Jade-green gazing ball.*

1

2

3

5

4

Grass gardens

GRASS GARDENS Modern man evolved from ancestors that walked the grasslands of Africa and feared the forest. Early civilization was dependent on managing and cultivating grasses – not only as grazing for domesticated animals like cattle, sheep and pigs, but as a nutritious staple in the form of bread to efficiently feed growing communities. Corn, wheat, barley, rye, oats and even rice are all species of nutritious grasses.

Grasses for ornamentation are a relatively recent phenomenon, valued for their graceful softening effect, particularly in mixed perennial borders where plants have a tendency to grow stiff, erect stems. The slender arching leaf blades of grasses produce movement, and many are sufficiently hardy to endure both harsh winters and dry summers. Some, like fescues, are evergreen, and even those that are deciduous will persist through winter with decorative dried amber leaves and flower plumes, gracing the snowy landscape.

Where a prairie effect is desired, such as a meadow garden, few grasses look better than little bluestem (*Schizachyrium scoparium*). Growing to four feet in height, it has blue-green erect leaves in summer, changing to pinkish-orange in autumn, and persisting through winter months. When back-lit, the orange leaf blades glow, a brightness that is intensified after a light dusting of frost or snow.

Hardy fountain grass (*Pennisetum alopecuroides*) is used extensively at Cedaridge Farm for its graceful leaf blades and

1 *Bamboo and arched footbridge.* 2 *Fountain grass spotlighted with shaft of light.* 3 *Rock garden featuring grasses, Cedaridge Farm.* 4 *Grasses surrounding pond, Cedaridge Farm.*

showy foxtail flowers. It's a good candidate for containers, especially when its large tuft of wispy leaf blades form the centerpiece, mingling with other foliage plants like coleus planted around the base.

The vast majority of ornamental grasses are perennial and prefer a sunny location, but there are some that tolerate light shade, such as Bowles golden sedge (*Carex elata* 'Bowles Golden'), and Japanese woodland grass (*Hakonechloa macra* 'Aureola'). Both these seem to shine with a golden glow, and Bowles golden sedge is even tolerant of boggy soil. Other colors that can be used in grass gardens include red Japanese blood grass (*Imperata cylindrical* 'Red Baron'), blue oat grass (*Helictotrichon sempervirens*), and silvery maiden grass (*Miscanthus sinensis* 'Variegatus').

When choosing grasses, consider whether the variety is clump-forming or spreading in habit. Clump-forming grasses like blue fescue will form a cushion of spiky leaves, staying neat and compact, while spreading types like variegated manna grass (*Glyceria maxima* 'Variegata') can be invasive, sending out tough underground shoots in all directions, but useful as a groundcover.

The extensive color palette of grasses, their rich array of heights and textures, their adaptability to a wide range of soil conditions, and the decorative flower plumes many provide, means that an entire garden can be planted with grasses and grass-like plants.

1 *Pampas plume highlights a grass garden.* 2 *Grasses flesh out a mixed border.* 3 *Japanese woodland grass softens a sunken garden.* 4 *House among tussock grasses.*

Grottoes

GROTTOES can take the form of a cave, a sheltered depression or an entrance to a tunnel. They are usually dark, moist places made of stone, often featuring a waterfall or natural spring where the acoustics of the cavern will eerily amplify sounds of dripping, gurgling and splashing. Existing caves are often transformed into grottoes by adding ornamentation, such as shell and mosaic patterns on the walls, statuary and water cascades. Tunnel grottoes are often connected to secret passageways, the entrance disguised with ferns and other moisture-loving plants to hide its real purpose of providing secret access to a building.

Grottoes constructed from stone or brick are usually placed along a stream or as a decorative accent in a bog garden, serving the practical purpose of providing a place to stay cool on hot, humid days.

In ancient times, grottoes were places to perform religious ceremonies, the Greeks using them to make offerings to nymphs, hence their name 'nymphaeum' for a grotto. In England and France, some grottoes were used for sacrificial ceremonies associated with devil worship and the occult. At Versailles Palace an elaborate grotto was constructed as a playground for Marie Antoinette, the last Queen of France, to play hide-and-seek with courtiers. The grottoes were connected by a labyrinth of subterranean passageways and each grotto entrance opened on to a pool. Streams feeding into the pond from the grottoes are criss-crossed with stepping stones and rustic bridges.

1 *Grotto almost hidden by gunnera, Kerdalo garden, Britanny.*
2 *Grotto at Blake House, California.* 3 *Grotto featuring statuary, Vatican Gardens.* 4 *Grotto at Villa Ile de France, near Nice.* 5 *Grotto at Nassau Botanical Garden, Bahamas.*

1

2

3

5

4

Groundcovers

GROUNDCOVERS are plants that create a dense weave of stems, roots and leaves to cover large expanses – especially slopes – and to control weeds. Choice depends on the site: sunny or shady, dry slopes or boggy ground. Usually an evergreen groundcover (like English ivy for a shady area, and creeping juniper for a sunny area) is preferred over deciduous kinds, presenting a permanent weed barrier through all the seasons.

Though most groundcovers are chosen for leaf color, texture and form, some provide the extra benefit of beautiful flowers, for example, osteospermum, ajuga and creeping phlox (*P. subulata*). Some are clump-forming and tend to stay within bounds (like hostas for shade and hen-and-chicks sedums for sun), while others spread by aggressive underground roots, for example yellow archangel (*Lamium galeobdolon*) and dwarf bamboo, becoming invasive within a few years if not controlled.

Some durable groundcovers for dry, sunny situations include bearberry (*Arctostaphylos uva-ursi*), creeping phlox, daylilies, grasses, heather, honeysuckle, hypericum, juniper, lamb's ears, lily-of-the-valley, mugo pine, sea pinks, sedum and sempervivum. For shade consider ajuga, bergenia, bunchberry (*Cotinus canadensis*), epimedium, ferns, hostas, ivies, lady's mantle, mondo grass, pachysandra, sweet woodruff and vinca.

Several good groundcovers are tough enough to stand foot traffic and offer fragrance when the leaves are bruised, including dwarf chamomile 'Treneague' and varieties of thyme.

1 *Evergreen ivy-covered cliff, Butchard Gardens, Canada.*
2 *Creeping juniper covers a boulder.* 3 *Floral clock using sedums for groundcover.* 4 *Perennial thyme edging a sunken path.* 5 *Perennial osteospermum covers a slope.* 6 *Black mondo grass surrounds pony-tail palms.* 7 *Drifts of perennial creeping phlox.*

1

7

6

2

3

4

5

Hanging baskets

HANGING BASKETS are a means of taking color high into the sky and also growing plants where natural soil is non-existent, such as a deck or patio. A big problem, however, is the tendency for baskets to dry out quickly compared to other containers. A mixture of commercial potting soil and garden topsoil, plus the addition of moisture-retentive crystals, will slow evaporation yet allow excess moisture to drain away. In soils that drain too quickly, hanging baskets may need watering twice a day. The worst baskets are plastic since they can overheat and burn delicate plant roots. The best tend to be made of wire and lined with sphagnum moss or coconut matting since they resist overheating.

Favorite places for hanging baskets are suspended from arbors and arches, also from the eves of a porch or veranda. They are also good for decorating a monotonous blank wall, attached to an L-shaped bracket, and can be mixed with window-box planters for a riotous display in such situations.

Some exceptional plants for baskets include 'Cascade' petunias, 'Balcan' ivy-leaf geraniums, and 'Whirligig' nasturtiums. For shade, consider 'Futura' basal-branching impatiens, cascading forms of tuberous begonias, and 'Penny' violas.

1

2

3

4

8   9

6   5

7

1 *Curtain of spider plants, pink verbena and blue plumbago, Conestoga House, Pennsylvania.* 2 *Slipper orchid basket.*
3 *Verbena basket.* 4 *Wall of mixed annuals in baskets.*
5 *Basket of mixed tuberous begonias.* 6 *Double-flowered impatiens basket.* 7 *Fuchsia basket.* 8 *Nasturtium basket.*
9 *Ivy-leaf geraniums in tiered baskets.*

Hedges

HEDGES are barriers or dividers made by closely spacing woody plants so their tight knit of branches weave together to make a continuous green wall. They are often better alternatives to walls and fences in a garden since they can be more soothing as a divider or barrier. Also, they invariably make a better background for flower borders. Indeed, hedges work better as a windbreak than either a wall or a fence, since they will cushion the force of winds and dissipate their strength, while more solid walls and fences will sometimes cause a high wind to jump over with even greater force. When a hedge is used as a windbreak it may need some protection to become established, such as a temporary screen of burlap sacking or straw bales placed on the windward side.

Slow-growing hedge plants like boxwood and yew will take time to become established, but then may need pruning only once during the growing season to keep their lines clean and sharp. Slow-growing plants are particularly desirable for low hedges such as those used in knot gardens and parterres, or for hedges incorporating topiaried features (page 189).

Good soil preparation is essential since hedge plants need to grow uniformly bushy and stay vigorous for many years. To achieve this it is advisable to dig a trench the length of the proposed hedge to a depth of at least 2 ft by 2 ft wide, and mix in some slow-release fertilizer and soil conditioner. Booster applications of fertilizer can be applied in autumn of each year.

1 *Common boxwood hedge.* 2 *Hemlock screening hedge.*
3 *Hemlock rondel at Sissinghurst Garden, UK.*
4 *Hedge of alternating azalea colors.*

1

2

4

3

Though evergreen woody plants are favorite hedge choices, certain deciduous trees and shrubs (such as beech and privet) will produce a sufficiently dense knit of branches to form an impenetrable barrier. Burning bush (*Euonymus*) and amur maple have the added benefit of beautiful autumn foliage colors; shrubs such as lilac and hydrangea also create hedges of seasonal charm.

Spacing to form a substantial hedge will depend on the type of woody plant used. For example, a spreading plant like weeping Atlas cedar can be spaced at least six feet apart, but more upright-growing plants like cherry laurel and holly will need spacing as close as three feet.

Certain plants can make a 'tapestry hedge' of alternating foliage color. Yellow, purple and green forms of berberis can achieve this, also green, blue and yellow forms of evergreen false cypress. Evergreen azaleas with their abundance of red, pink and white spring blossoms can make a beautiful flowering hedge.

1

4

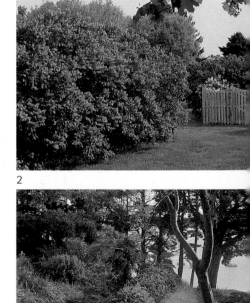

2

3

1 *Hemlock hedge with topiary swan, Ladew Topiary Garden, Maryland.* 2 *Lilac hedge.* 3 *Hydrangea hedge, Port Blanc, Britanny.* 4 *Common yew hedge, Powys Castle, Wales.*

Herb gardens

HERB GARDENS are more challenging to create than most other theme gardens, for many useful herbs have insignificant flowers and a weedy appearance when seen individually so we must compensate with an imaginative design that emphasizes subtle qualities, such as plant habit and the shape, color and texture of the leaves. Also, it is often the layout of the design, such as a pattern of low hedges and a grid of radiating paths, that helps to make an herb garden attractive. As a general rule, highly formal designs for herb gardens are more appealing than informal designs, which can look untidy if not maintained scrupulously.

In ancient civilizations and as recently as colonial times, herb gardens were an essential part of life, producing flavors to make food palatable, and deodorizing scents to disguise household odors before the advent of modern plumbing. Herbs were also grown as a source of dye, as effective insect repellents, and as a medicine (such as mints to relieve sinus congestion). When an herb garden is devoted to medicinal plants it is often called a 'physic' or 'physick garden'. The most famous of these is the Chelsea Physick Garden, a four-acre property beside the River Thames. London's oldest botanical garden, founded in 1673 for the study of plants, today it features some 5000 plant species. Its sheltered position between tall buildings and the river provides it with a micro-climate that allows the growing of Mediterranean olive trees, and other tender plants, outdoors.

1 Medieval herb garden, The Cloisters, New York. 2 Physic garden, University of British Columbia, Canada. 3 Herbal knot garden, Cleveland Botanical Garden, Ohio. 4 Herb garden with beehive at Chicago Botanical Garden, Illinois.

1

2

4

3

Today, herbs are grown mostly to supply flavorings for the kitchen and often combined with vegetables in the one plot. When planning a functional herb garden one should take into consideration that you don't need a lot of any particular herb since their flavors are concentrated and often a small bunch of leaves is sufficient to flavor a meal. Even so, some herbs do possess beautiful flowers, and though the majority of their edible leaves may never be harvested, it's worth planting a good number to provide floral color. For example, the pink globular flowerheads of chives are outstanding in spring. Similarly, varieties of thyme, lavender, bergamot and dill are well worth growing in abundance for floral effect, with fragrance and culinary value an added bonus.

Most herbs demand a well-drained soil in a sunny location. In general, herbs are drought tolerant, will survive in impoverished soil, and may rot if over-watered. Some (like mints and bergamot) can be exceedingly aggressive, and so it may be best to confine them to beds of their own or, better still, a pot rather than allow them to run rampant.

The most popular formal herb garden design is a quadrant. Quadrants are simply a square or rectangular shape, divided into four planting compartments by intersecting paths, usually of brick. Cartwheel designs are also popular, with low dividing fences or hedges radiating out from a central hub like the spokes of a wheel. At the center can be a pedestal, bee skep or other decorative accent. Knot gardens are the most elaborate of herb garden designs, and the most labor intensive, for the miniature hedges defining the pattern must be kept clean and neat by timely pruning.

Throughout the world many commercial establishments – notably gourmet restaurants and historic hotels – feature elaborate herb gardens. One of the finest herbal knot gardens is at Bodysgallen – 'The House of Thistles' – a hotel-spa in North Wales. The intricate medieval parterre design is from English boxwood, with herbs of different colors and textures planted between the hedges. The Ballymaloe Inn and Cookery School in Ireland is renowned for its mostly rectangular beds, edged with germander and filled with useful culinary herbs in contrasting colors, in a layout inspired by the vegetable parterres at Villandry, France.

Herb gardens are appropriate for ecclesiastical buildings. The Cloisters, located in Fort Tyron Park, New York City, is

1

7

6

5

1 *Cauvin Lavender Farm, Provence.* 2 *Combination herb/vegetable garden.* 3 *Quadrant herb garden.* 4 *Herb garden, Larnach Castle, New Zealand.* 5 *Herb garden at Inverewe, Scotland.* 6 *Mints with antique hand pump.* 7 *Herb garden at Cranbrook House, USA.*

2

4

3

a replica of a European monastery, the stones shipped to New York from demolished monasteries in France and Germany. Opened in 1938, the building is part of the Metropolitan Art Museum, and houses a collection of valuable medieval art. The Cuxa Cloister features a quadrant herb garden with a fountain at its center and the Bonnefont Cloister has a Venetian wellhead as its focal point. A third cloister, the Trie, features European wildflowers and herbs.

Because herbs are required in relatively small amounts for flavoring meals, many are suitable for growing in pots, which can make good use of a small space such as a sunny deck or patio. In recent years there has been a startling interest in basils, to such an extent that a special area of the herb garden can feature a wide selection, from dwarf to tall varieties, green foliaged and bronze foliaged, and some with such beautiful pink flower clusters they can be grown among annuals in flower gardens.

Of all flowering herbs, undoubtedly the most popular is English lavender. It is the hardiest of lavenders, and will bloom continuously for most of the summer, its spiky flowers producing a blue haze. All parts are delightfully fragrant and useful in numerous ways – to scent bathwater, placed beside a pillow to scent a bedroom, steeped in boiling water to make a refreshing tea or distilled into oil to perfume soaps and other cosmetics. The variety 'Hidcote' has the deepest blue coloring, though the variety 'Munstead' is hardier. Lavender can be planted in regimented rows to simulate the lavender farms of Provence, such as the Cauvin Lavender Farm, near La Pouldu, where a nature trail to the castle ruins of Châteauneuf-du-Pape provides spectacular views to France's Alpes Maritime, the valleys cloaked in wild lavender.

1 *Herb parterre garden at Pitmedden, Scotland.* 2 *Herb knot garden at Clos Coudray, France.* 3 *Sundial herb garden, Cedaridge Farm.*

Hillsides

HILLSIDES are usually excellent places on which to landscape a garden because many levels of interest can be arranged in a relatively small space, with room for a variety of structural features so the walk up and down the hillside becomes a visually exciting adventure. Hillsides can include streams and waterfalls, pools, observation platforms, belvederes, steps, zig-zag paths, terraces, retaining walls, rocky outcrops, arches, grottoes, generous sweeps of groundcovers, balustrades, and many other structures.

Remember that with a hillside the views looking up can be as stimulating as those looking down. If erosion might be a problem (such as with sandy or shale slopes), then consider stabilizing the slope with a series of retaining walls and terraces, using good topsoil to back fill behind the walls for plants to become established. With a gentle slope, paths can lead directly down from one planting area to another, creating a strong axis, but on steep slopes a stairway may be necessary. Where a slope is too steep for a path and steps too costly to install, paths can zig-zag downhill for comfort and safety.

Take advantage of the natural contours of the hillside to determine where to place ornamental features. For example, identify places where water run-off is concentrated. Perhaps it has already formed a shallow gully where a stream and waterfalls can be established. If the slope levels out in places, consider these as ideal spots to establish an observation platform, deck or belvedere.

1 Matai Moana coastal garden, New Zealand. 2 Steps edged with Japanese maples. 3 Terraces at Gethsemane Garden, New Zealand. 4 Maple Glen garden, New Zealand.

1

2

4

3

If there are tall trees obscuring a view of distant countryside or coastal features, resist cutting them down to improve the view. Instead, consider pruning away lower branches leaving a topknot of foliage, so the trunks become pillars you can see through.

Also, consider generous drifts of ground-hugging plants – especially those that will spread and spill over rock outcrops and retaining walls, since colonies of low-growing plants can look more natural than individuals spotted randomly. If there are existing boulders, landscape around them rather than pay for heavy earthmoving equipment to shift them.

In coastal locations find out from local garden centers what plants are considered wind- and salt-tolerant, since there is nothing more disheartening than to pay for beautiful healthy specimens, only to see them suffer browning and deterioration from wind and salt burn.

1 *Pukemara hillside garden, New Zealand.* 2 *Main house overlooking Cobamong garden, New York State.* 3 *Hillside garden, Attadale, Scotland.* 4 *Main axis, Pukemarama garden, New Zealand.*

1

4

2

3

Islamic gardens

ISLAMIC GARDENS 'On the great plain of Marvadascht east of the Zagros Mountains lie the scattered remains of the earliest garden of which we have a record,' begins Penelope Hobhouse in her book, *The Gardens of Persia* (2004). Established in 550 BC by Cyrus the Great to commemorate a victorious battle, the ruins are of a formal walled garden. The white columns of a pavilion, for entertaining, remain upright, and excavations suggest that the layout was a quadrangular design, the quadrants dissected with water channels that irrigated plantings of fruit trees such as almond, fig and pomegranate. A dominant water channel forms a central axis, with a circular pool at its center.

Persian gardens date to at least 3000 BC, and were the inspiration for the Koran, in which it is decreed that gardens are a foretaste of heaven to come, and thus Persian gardens served as a prototype for the Islamic garden.

The site for Cyrus the Great's garden is desert, but thirty miles away are the foothills of the Zagros Mountains where snow melt drains into subterranean water tables. A series of underground conduits tapped the water table and directed a flow of water to irrigate Cyrus the Great's garden and fill his grid of water channels and circular pool.

Islam spread to India in the east and Morocco in the west, where gardens were modeled on the Persian original of quadrants and multiple quadrants. When the Moroccans (Moors) conquered most of Spain they established Islamic gardens as part of their governing palaces, and even after the expulsion of the Moors, the Islamic influence remained strong in subsequent Spanish garden designs in the New World as well as areas around the French and Italian Riviera.

In Britain today, the garden of Sezincote, Gloucestershire, was transformed by Lady Kleinwort into an Islamic garden. The main house not only features an 'onion dome' but is notable for minarets, balconies and windows in the Islamic Indian style. The main lawn vista includes a quadrant design with a water channel and pool forming the central axis.

In the USA, the New Orleans plantation garden of Longue View, developed by the late Mr. and Mrs. Edgar B. Stern, includes a number of Islamic design features. A Spanish Court, inspired by a visit to the Alhambra Palace and Generalife Gardens in Spain, has water channels with arching jets and scalloped fountains.

1 *Spanish/Moorish-style courtyard, Carmel Mission, Carmel, California.* 2 *Moorish courtyard garden, Menton, France.* 3 *Moorish courtyard garden, Arles, France.*

Italian gardens

ITALIAN GARDENS are undoubtedly among the world's most ostentatious gardens, the best surviving examples dating to the Rennaissance in the 17th and 18th centuries, when their sumptuous vistas, fantastic fountains and splendid statuary inspired such vainglorious imitations as Vaux-le-Vicomte and Versailles Palace, in France, also Chatsworth in England, plus Hearst Castle, California, and Villa Viscaya, in Florida.

Gardens like those at the Vatican and homes of Vatican cardinals such as Villa d'Este and Villa Lante – all of them near Rome – set the standard for an exuberant style and ornate ornamentation that has become known as baroque, from the Italian *baroquismo*.

The late Edith Wharton, the Pulitzer prizewinning American writer, described the Villa d'Este as a musical organ on which water is played, calling it 'extraordinarily beautiful and romantic', while Villa Lante, for its restrained ostentation, she described as 'So perfect...far does it surpass in beauty, in preservation, and in the quality of the garden-magic, all the other pleasure houses of Italy.' The late Carlton B. Lees, American garden writer and garden historian, agreed with Wharton's assessment of Villa Lante, writing, 'If Villa Lante is "perfect moderation" then Villa d'Este is perfect ostentation.' Lees believed that when Cardinal Ippolito d'Este II was appointed governor of Tivoli in 1550 and bought an old Benedictine convent for his home, he pulled out all the stops, and created the most spectacular of the early villas of the Italian Renaissance. 'The architect, Pirro Ligorio, put together for the cardinal such a monumental ensemble of fountains, jets, cascades, pools, ponds, waterfalls, sprays and gurgles that even in brilliant sunlight of 20th century high noon, Villa d'Este seems more fantasy than reality,' Lees concluded.

One of the finest examples of a small-space Italianate garden outside Italy is at Blake House, Kensington, California, now owned by the University of California, Berkeley. Established by Anita Blake and Mabel Symmes, a landscape graduate from Berkeley, the house dates to the 1820s and overlooks the city of San Francisco. The heart of the garden is a long, narrow reflecting pool bordered by Southern evergreen magnolias. Though shaded by these, the pool receives sufficient light to grow water lilies, the length and narrowness of the pool leading the eye like an arrow to a handsome pair of sweeping stone stairs that ascend to a balcony above a grotto.

1 *Terrace above the clouds, Hearst Castle, California.*
2 *Parterres at Vatican gardens.* 3 *Fountain and umbrella pines, Vatican gardens.* 4 *Italianate garden, Blake House, California.*

Japanese gardens

JAPANESE GARDENS, outside of Japan, can look out of place because there is a temptation for gardeners to confuse Japanese with Chinese, and also to create a discordant Westernized hybrid of pseudo-Japanese elements. In actuality, traditional Japanese gardens took inspiration from Chinese meditation gardens, but then became more refined, using less animated ornamentation. For example, dragons and limestone boulders pitted like Swiss cheese – so prevalent in Chinese gardens – are not authentic to Japanese gardens. Indeed, *shibusa*, the Japanese word for quiet and refined taste, describes the chief characteristics of Japanese gardens which seek to provide a feeling of serenity, nobility, conservatism, introspection and reserve – the antithesis of anything loud, noisy, garish or bizarre.

The earliest historical reference to a garden in Japan describes the design of a miniature mountain landscape for the Empress Suiko in AD606. Besides an artificial hill, the garden contained a lake, the shoreline of which represented a section of rugged coast, with rocks arranged to create inlets and promontories crowned with windswept, contorted pines.

Josiah Condor, author of *Landscape Gardening in Japan* (1893), was an architect who studied Japanese landscape design while teaching architecture at the Imperial University, Tokyo. His book includes a history of Japanese garden development, and discusses the significance of design elements such as garden stones, lanterns, pagodas, water basins, enclosures, wells, bridges, arbors, use of water, plantings and five kinds of popular garden: hillside, lakeside, ceremonial, passageways, and fantasy. 'A garden in Japan is a representation of

1–3 Autumn scenes from Swiss Pines Japanese Garden, Pennsylvania, featuring tower, bridge and basin as ornamental accents.

1

2

3

the scenery of the country,' he explained. 'The artificial hills, rocks, lakes, torrent beds, and cascades of gardens are copied from striking features in the varied landscape of the country.' The natural compositions of dry riverbeds, weathered trees, the outlines of mountains and hills, are all closely studied by Japanese garden designers, who often render deliberate exaggerations, for example, using skilful pruning to re-create weathered tree forms. Their expressiveness in bringing nature into the garden is rather like the popular painting technique, Impressionism, which is an artist's exaggeration of nature in order to express what is in his heart, his inner eye.

Hence, Japanese gardens are full of symbolism using basically water, stones and evergreen plants. Mossy mounds can represent a line of hills, boulders among gravel can depict islands along a stony shore. Running water becomes the music of nature and still water, introduced to make a mirror, doubles the beauty of its surroundings. The Japanese understand the many moods of water – alluringly beautiful when clear and filled with the flashing images of fish, yet hauntingly mysterious when it is dark and opaque.

When Monet decided to create a water garden after planting his Clos Normand flower garden, he made it as he envisioned a Japanese garden after talking to Japanese experts and reading about Japanese garden design. He constructed a Japanese-style bridge at one end as a focal point, and then hired a Japanese nurseryman to advise him on the importation of Japanese plants to make his water garden authentic, not only establishing colonies of familiar Japanese plants like bamboo and water irises, but also important unfamiliar ones like tree peonies and Japanese butterbur (*Petasites japonicus*), with large heart-shaped leaves.

In a Japanese garden the balance of plants should be two-thirds evergreen and one-third deciduous to establish a sense of permanence and greenery during the bleakness of winter. Where Japanese camellia shrubs are not sufficiently hardy for a garden, then a hardy American *Franklinia* tree or Chinese *Stewartia* might be substituted. 'It is not necessary to use only authentic Japanese plants to create a Japanese garden,' insists Japanese Zen garden master, Hiroshi Makita. 'It is the spirit we must create, and if certain Japanese plants are not adaptable, it is better to select native trees and shrubs well-suited to the area.'

The Japanese garden masters favor plants that look beautiful in autumn and winter, as well as spring and summer. Japanese thread-leaf maples are prized for their intense russet colors in autumn and for the beauty of their bare branch silhouettes in winter, especially when the canopy is covered with a light dusting of snow.

Water in Japanese gardens takes on many forms: a rocky stream, a tumbling cascade, a quiet pool, even a hollowed stone with a catchment of rainwater in which to float an azalea blossom. There are 'smooth' and 'broken' falls and myriad gradations in between.

1

2 3

4

5 6

7

1 *Japanese wooden footbridge.*
2 *Japanese tower in snow.* 3 *Katsura Imperial Villa garden, Kyoto.* 4 *Katsura Imperial Villa garden, Kyoto.* 5 *Tower, bridge and frog sculpture along a stream.* 6 *Turf bridge, Japanese garden, Brenthurst garden, Johannesburg.*
7 *Lantern at Swiss Pines Japanese Garden, Pennsylvania.* 8 *Spring foliage in the Japanese garden, Seattle Arboretum.*

Color must not be garish, but understated, and though there are splashes of color at special times, the flowering plant palette is generally composed of a few plant species: cherry blossoms massed to briefly display a blizzard of pink and white blossoms in early spring; colonies of blue and purple Japanese water irises along stream and pond margins in summer; and in autumn sheets of red, orange and yellow from a leaf canopy composed of mostly Japanese maples and ginkgos.

Zen masters also like to include a strong sense of human presence in their designs – for example, well-defined paths, rustic bridges, chunky benches, rough stepping stones, and shelters.

The five gardens in Japan considered to be the best examples of traditional Japanese garden art are all in Kyoto. Three are Imperial gardens: the Katsura Detached Imperial Villa (noted for its beautifully landscaped fish pond), the Sento Palace stroll garden (famous for its immense pebble beach comprised of charcoal-gray stones hand-selected to be identical in shape and size), and the Shugakuin Imperial Villa stroll garden (with an immense stone bridge connecting the mainland to a pavilion on an island). The other two, also in Kyoto, are the Ryoan-ji Temple Garden (famed for its meditative rock and gravel garden), and the Saiho-ji Temple Garden, famous for its moss.

Because of the large number of Japanese immigrants to North America, there are some superb Japanese gardens there. Both Seattle and Portland have large Japanese gardens carefully maintained to ensure authenticity. A gem of a Japanese garden exists near Philadelphia. Known as Swiss Pines for the number of these trees that used to grow here, the garden has had several landscape architects working on its construction, including Hiroshi Makita. It emulates a Japanese stroll garden, with a meandering path taking visitors on a visual adventure through a valley coursed by a small stream that enters the property as a waterfall and descends to its lowest level via a series of cascades and ponds. A unique design element is the rainbow garden wherein a bamboo water spout arches a stream of water over a path and down a cliff face, to splash on rocks thirty feet below. On sunny days, as the water splinters in a fine spray on the rocks, a double rainbow is formed!

1 *Japanese garden at Welcome Farm, Pennsylvania.* 2 *Japanese garden at Museum of Modern Art, Boston.* 3 *Japanese garden, Cedaridge Farm.* 4 *Japanese irises in the Japanese Garden, Portland, Oregon.*

Knot gardens

KNOT GARDENS began to appear in Britain in the 15th century after the idea of hedge patterns became popular in Italian Renaissance gardens, and spread to France, where the French made them more elaborate and called them parterres. Owners of French chateaux liked the idea of being able to look down from an upstairs window at an elaborate design of scrolls and flourishes, highlighted by colored gravel or bedding plants between the lines. Whereas Italian boxwood hedges were mostly geometric with a criss-cross pattern, the French made them look like embroidery.

The British took the idea a step further to create patterns that resembled ribbons tied in knots, making part of the hedge pattern uniform, but where the hedges intersected, there would be a change in height and width, even producing a mounded form to make the knot more realistic.

Also, rather than restricting the hedges to boxwood, the British used more than one plant to suggest several strands entwined. Thus, a knot garden might use green boxwood, bronze-leaf barberry, silvery lavender, blue dwarf juniper and golden sage.

Knot gardens do not need to be large to look impressive. Dwarf forms of germander, barberry and boxwood allow knot hedges to remain low and compact. These dwarf forms are especially useful to create small herb gardens, using varieties of culinary herbs exclusively to form the knots.

1 *Knot garden at Gethsemane Garden, New Zealand.*
2 *Sage and lavender cotton knot.* 3 *Boxwood and berberis knot.*
4 *Knot garden at Filoli garden, California.* 5 *Medieval knot garden, Bodysgallen estate, Wales.*

5

4

Labels and signs

LABELS AND SIGNS are a necessary evil in most gardens – labels to identify plants for the inquisitive visitor and signs to identify the entrance to a show garden, provide historical information about a plant or garden space, and other essential data, including suggested viewing route and the location of the lavatories.

Plant labels can look hideous, for example shiny aluminum squares on which a name is scratched with a scribe, and hung from branches with a twist-tie, or stuck into the ground on a wire holder.

At Cedaridge Farm, pieces of T-shaped slate are used to identify plants, the name written in white, with a tiny painting of the plant. These labels are costly, but they last forever. The Bagatelle Rose Garden, Paris, has a particularly stylish label to identify its roses: a piece of oval porcelain with the name lettered in black, the porcelain mounted in a metal frame onto wire legs that can be pushed firmly into the ground or twisted around a branch.

1 *A whimsical statement to produce a pause and a smile in a cottage garden.*
2 *A durable slate label.* 3 *A dignified porcelain plant label, Bagatelle Gardens, France.* 4, 5, 6 and 7 *Signs identifying a property, garden or place.*

Lakes

LAKES 'A view is worth a thousand flowers, a lake is worth ten thousand,' wrote the owner of one of England's largest estate gardens, Robin Loder, when describing the charm of his woodland garden, Leonardslee, in Sussex.

As well as providing an inviting place to sail a boat, fish or swim, a large stretch of calm water can add inestimable beauty to any property, reflecting sunrises, sunsets and seasonal changes in the surrounding countryside. Not everyone has the space for a lake, but those who do should realize that there are three qualities that can help to make it beautiful: exquisite reflections, a rim of trees and framing elements at the approach to the lake so extraneous elements are screened out. Providing they are framed well, with mature clumps of trees and shrubs reflected in the water, lakes often require little embellishment. Perhaps nowhere in the world is this more evident than at Magnolia Plantation, South Carolina, where tannin from the roots of cypress trees stains the lake's water black, and produces a highly reflective surface. This reflective quality causes myriad visual sensations: glittering and shimmering with the slightest gust of wind, a mirror-smooth surface allowing waterlilies to grow and swans to float regally to and fro, the surface dancing with ripples from raindrops on rainy days.

The most beautiful of all English garden lakes is Stourhead, Wiltshire, made by banker Henry Hoare damming the River Stour in the 1740s. This allowed him to create one major lake and several smaller ones. Around these he planted mostly native trees, selecting ones that would look especially beautiful in the autumn, including oaks, beech and conifers. Gentle dips and slopes covered in lawn hold back the woodland in places and provide views of classical monuments strategically placed around the lake's margin: a domed, colonnaded structure called the Pantheon (a scaled-down replica of the Pantheon in Rome), two temples, and a beautiful arched stone bridge. The buildings, the trees, the contours of the land and the sloping lawns all contrast with the smooth surface of the water.

Of course there is some confusion over definitions, and whether to describe a body of water as a lake or a pond. Walden Pond in Massachusetts, for example, would be considered a lake in most other countries.

1

2

4   3

1 *Lake at Nemours garden, Delaware, in autumn.* 2 *Lake at Magnolia Plantation, South Carolina.* 3 *Lake at Thorndale garden, New York state.* 4 *Lake at Rathmoy garden, New Zealand.*

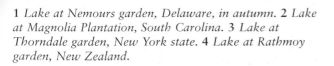

Lathe houses

LATHE HOUSES are structures of upright beams with a slatted roof, open on all sides, normally for the purpose of providing a shady area for houseplants to be parked during frost-free months. They are also used for growing collections of shade-loving plants like ferns, tuberous begonias and fuchsias. Lathe houses are especially suitable for holding flats of seedlings and rooted cuttings prior to being transplanted, particularly shade-loving plants like wax begonias, colcus and hostas.

In frost-free areas a lathe house can be used for growing shade-loving orchids and shade-loving epiphytic cacti like epiphyllum, with blooms sometimes the size of dinner plates. The slats providing shade are good to hang baskets from.

Lathe houses can also do double duty as sitting areas since the cooling shade can be a pleasant place to escape summer heat. Remember, too, that the outstretched limbs of a mature tree often can substitute for a lathe structure.

1 *Lathe house for fuchsia baskets.* 2 *Lathe house for begonia baskets.* 3 *Lathe house for raising seedlings.* 4 *Lathe house with fountain and orchid collection.*

1

2

3

4

Lawns

LAWNS can be formal in shape or informal, established by seeding, sodding with squares of turf or plugging with grasses that spread by tillering. Lawns are most suitable for sunny locations to create an expanse of green that is restful on the eye and less maintenance than having the same space devoted to flowerbeds or a vegetable plot, but not as labor-saving as a durable perennial groundcover such as English ivy or liriope.

Some of the most appealing lawns are sunken, or bowl-shaped to create a depression around a fountain, or even an amphitheater around a stage for outdoor entertainment.

An often overlooked benefit of having a lawn is the potential for beautiful shadow patterns. By placing a lawn where tall trees will cast their shadows over it at sunrise or sunset, the splendor of a greensward can truly be appreciated, like the tiered lawn at Middleton Place, South Carolina, which pencils strong shadows down a sloping lawn sandwiched between lakes whenever the sun is low on the horizon.

Bluegrass and perennial ryegrass are popular lawn grasses for sunny locations, while fine fescue is more desirable for light shade. Salt-tolerant bentgrass is valued for coastal locations and where a fine putting-green appearance is desired.

1 *Formal lawn and tulip borders, Dumbarton Oaks, Washington DC.* 2 *Freeform lawn and annual borders, Butchard Gardens, Canada.* 3 *Circular lawn behind a suburban home.*

1

2

3

Seeding is the least expensive way to establish a new lawn compared to sodding (the purchase of ready-grown turf from a turf or sod farm). The cost of purchasing turf, transporting it to the site and laying it in place will be much higher.

Plug-type lawns are mostly composed of zoysia, St. Augustine grass and similar grasses that spread sideways by underground roots called tillers. The plugs are planted 12 inches apart and they eventually knit together to create a weed-suffocating turf. However, zoysia goes dormant after frost and though the roots will remain viable, the top-growth turns an unsightly brown until frost-free days return in spring. Moreover, the plugs can take up to two years to make a thick turf cover. Plug-type grasses are best for subtropical and tropical locations where they can remain green year-round.

For optimum results, a lawn should be seeded as a mixture. For example, a good all-purpose lawn mixture might contain 20 percent improved perennial ryegrass, 70 percent bluegrass and 10 percent fine fescue. In a sunny location the improved perennial ryegrass will germinate first – within three days under ideal conditions – and in ten days the bluegrass will germinate to fill in any bare spots where the perennial ryegrass has failed. If there are any shady areas that inhibit

1 *Undulating lawn, Oehme Gardens, Washington State.*
2 *Freeform lawn, coastal garden, California.* 3 *Freeform lawn with rhododendron borders.* 4 *Circular lawn and perennial border.* 5 *Freeform lawn with mixed borders.*
6 *Fragrant chamomile lawn.* 7 *Horseshoe-shaped brick path with lawn centerpiece.*

1

7

6

2

3

4

5

the germination of the improved perennial ryegrass and the bluegrass, the shade-tolerant fine fescue will establish itself.

In deep shade, where grasses will not grow, shade-tolerant groundcovers like *Vinca minor* and *Pachysandra terminalis* should be considered.

Alternatives to grass in sunny areas, especially on slopes where grass can be difficult to grow, are chamomile and thyme, which require no mowing. Both chamomile and thyme are naturally drought tolerant, and they will endure a moderate amount of foot traffic. An advantage to both is that when stepped upon, the leaves are bruised and release a spicy perfume. The color range of thyme, from white through pale pink to deep purple, allows several varieties to be grown in drifts to produce a patchwork quilt effect.

No-mow lawns such as thyme and chamomile can be grown using low-growing grasses that are allowed to develop to their natural height. Dwarf forms of blue fescue, such as 'Elijah Blue', and dwarf forms of carex, such as 'Frosty Curls' – both of which are hardy and clump-forming – are sufficiently uniform to produce a lawn effect without tedious mowing, though they are not suitable for playing lawn games because of the uneven surface.

1

1 *Circular lawn with shadows.* **2** *Lawn vista with shadows.*
3 *Lawn with perennial border at Inverewe Garden, Scotland.*

2

3

Light

LIGHT is even more important to plant growth than water or soil nutrients, for many plants can survive long periods of drought and impoverished soil, but with absence of light they soon perish. Indeed, a one percent increase in light can result in a one hundred percent increase in plant performance, which is why the removal of a single tree limb over a shaded site can make the difference between abundant bloom and no flowers at all. Even painting a dark background surface white, or using white stones to reflect light up into foliage, can make a significant difference in plant performance. The presence of a residence can produce different degrees of light intensity, southern exposures offering the best light and often creating a micro-climate in which borderline tender plants can thrive.

When sunlight floods a garden after a long period of rain or cloudy weather, a magical transformation can take place – new flowers open, petals glow with color, evocative silhouettes appear, and foliage that is back-lit will glow like a Chinese lantern – a quality keenly observed by Claude Monet, who preferred single flowers over doubles because flowers with a single row of petals, like cosmos, produce a transluscence that contributed to the glittering sensation he sought for his garden.

The light-reflective quality of surfaces is very important to Zen garden masters, for example smooth, charcoal-gray cobblestones are valued because after a shower of rain their color shines like ebony. Moreover, sites where morning mist can imbue the garden with muted colors were favored over sunnier sites, which is what attracted Monet to his property at Giverny, where mist from a nearby swamp and the River Seine was almost always present in his garden during early morning when he liked to paint. Gertrude Jekyll enjoyed planting golden gardens where a path emerged from shadow because even on a cloudy day, on entering her golden garden, she would feel as though she was stepping into an oasis of sunlight.

Artificial lighting allows a garden to be appreciated at night, and the styles of lighting available can be bewildering. Of particular benefit to gardeners are spotlights, either white or colored, to shine against structures such as a statue so the shadow from front-lighting is cast on a wall, or to dramatically silhouette a tree through back-lighting its trunk and spreading branches. The important point is to be selective and know what to highlight so there is a bold contrast between what is lit and what is dark (the Impressionist contrast of black and white). Isolated tree trunks with radiating branches might be good to silhouette, or the contorted branches of a Camperdown elm, or the coiling branches of the hazel known as Harry Lauder's walking stick (*Corylus avellana* 'Contorta') Also, small footlights are good for marking trails so a tour of the garden can be taken on moonlit nights or when glowworms and lightning bugs are an attraction. At Cedaridge Farm lightning bugs rise from the damp banks of a stream during summer, while glowworms can be see by the hundreds coiled up on top of leaf mold along a woodland path. The glowworm garden in particular is a favorite with children.

1 *Lake at Magnolia Plantation, South Carolina, in mist.*
2 *Backlit cosmos.* 3 *Backlit Spanish moss, Pine Mountain, Florida.* 4 *Morning shafts of light, Cedaridge Farm.*

Mazes and labyrinths

MAZES AND LABYRINTHS Though turf labyrinths date back to medieval and even pagan times, when patterns with religious symbolism were cut into turf or laid out with stones, the first hedge maze is believed to be the one at Hampton Court, near London. Laid out in the reign of King William III, circa 1700, when he resided at Hampton Court, the construction is credited to two of his gardeners, named London and Wise. Its design, in the shape of a shield, is a third of an acre in size, with half a mile of walkways. Made from English holly, it has been replicated at Colonial Williamsburg, Virginia; at Magnolia Plantation, South Carolina; and at Deerfield Garden, near Philadelphia. Planted by the late Tom Hallowell Jr., the Deerfield maze is especially good to study because it is a half-size replica of the Hampton Court maze, and made from English boxwood, which can be trimmed to make a sharper outline than English holly.

The Deerfield maze contains 1600 plants, and receives no special care except for an annual trimming before new growth begins in spring. Trimming is done every year with electric hedge shears, the whole process taking thirty-two hours. The Deerfield maze is maintained at about 48 inches in height, since the pattern can be seen by most standing adults. Children can wander the narrow, leafy passages of the Deerfield maze, and enjoy the excitement of getting thoroughly lost, while adults can peer over the hedges and find the center without much difficulty. Rooted cuttings 6 inches high were used to plant the maze, and it has taken forty years to reach the current stage of maturity, because of boxwood's slow natural growth rate of only 1 inch a year. Faster growing arborvitae, holly, yew, beech and hemlock are more popular choices for mazes, though they lack the dense foliage cover of English boxwood.

The site of the maze at Deerfield has proven so suitable that no fertilizing or watering has been necessary to keep it healthy, only mulching with shredded pine bark each spring. Still, the making of a hedge maze is considered one of the most challenging of horticultural endeavors.

1

2

4

3

1 Deerfield maze in snow, Pennsylvania. 2 Governor's Palace maze, Colonial Williamsburg. 3 Labyrinth path, Winterthur garden, Delaware. 4 Deerfield maze in spring.

Meadows

MEADOWS can feature closely-cropped grass and be made to look like a site for sheep (even stocked with live animals grazing inside a low stone wall or split-rail fence) or these areas can consist of uncut, arching grass blades mixed with vibrant colonies of wildflowers. Though a longlasting display can be orchestrated by planting wildflower species to bloom at different times, the most beautiful effects can be achieved by concentrating on a particular species, such as Texas bluebonnets (a type of lupin), or California poppies, both of which flower in spring.

The difficulty in establishing an uncut meadow is the tendency for indigenous weeds and aggressive native grasses to choke out desirable flowering plants. Generally, indigenous wildflowers are more successful at competing with weed growth than introduced varieties, and so one way to avoid weed competition is to create islands of good topsoil for seeding with quick-growing annuals like poppies and cornflowers. Since weed growth is less aggressive in autumn than it is in spring, a favorite time for seeding a meadow is the onset of the cool, rainy autumn season, allowing annuals to germinate and establish a crown of foliage before freezing weather makes them dormant.

1

1 *Drifts of creeping phlox, Connecticut.* 2 *Drifts of daffodils, Pennsylvania.* 3 *Prairie garden, Cedaridge Farm.* 4 *Swamp sunflower meadow, Cedaridge Farm.*

2

3

4

Mirrors and trompe l'oeil

MIRRORS AND TROMPE L'OEIL Mirrors are often used in small gardens to create a reflection and produce the illusion of greater distance, for example at the end of a small side garden in the city. The illusion works best if the reflection can show an extension of perspective, such as a straight path flanked by foliage.

Trompe l'oeil is a French term meaning 'to deceive the eye', to describe a device normally placed on walls to create a false impression of perspective, and therefore great depth. The deception can be created by an arrangement of latticework against a flat surface, the lattice made to look like a receding trellised arbor, or the illusion can be provided by a life-like mural, done in photo-realism style, of a garden space or a scenic view. These realistic views work particularly well when the foreground space is shady, and the trompe l'oeil mural is framed by an arch.

1 *Trompe l'oeil trelliswork, Nemours garden, Delaware.*
2 *Mirror used to provide illusion of distance.* 3 *Mirror disguised as a window, Cedaridge Farm.* 4 *Trompe l'oeil design on a wall.*

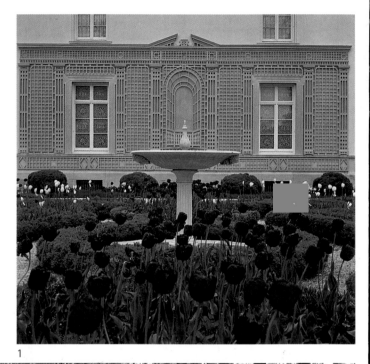

1

4

3

2

Mosaics and pebble designs

MOSAICS AND PEBBLE DESIGNS Though square and rectangular pieces of mosaic are available from home-supply stores, broken pieces of colored crockery, glass bottles and roofing tile make good substitutes. The masters of mosaic designs are the Moroccans, whose mosaic and tile gardens influenced Spanish garden design. In Morocco mosaic is used extensively in courtyard gardens, not only as edging to fountains, steps and paving, but also on walls.

Pebble designs using different shapes and colors of smooth beach pebbles can make a good substitute for mosaic tile, as do flat, slate-like pebbles used on edge, and shells (see page 164). Pebbles of different shapes and colors can substitute for mosaic tile in all manner of hardscape design, including steps, paths, fountains, paving and walls.

1 *Narrow mosaic path.* 2 *Pebble mosaic, Chinese design.*
3 *Spanish style mosaic steps.* 4 *Pebble mosaic, Chinese style.* 5 *Wall mosaic.* 6 *Islamic style fountain with mosaic design, Morocco.*

1

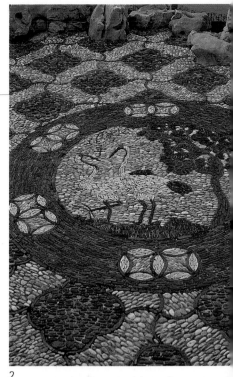

2

3

6

5

4

Moss gardens

MOSS GARDENS can be extremely difficult to maintain unless several environmental factors contribute to the establishment of mossy plants, including a highly acid soil, dappled shade, and a moisture-laden atmosphere. Moss has a hard time competing with weeds, and will not take heavy foot traffic, but for a lightly shaded woodland with a stream running through, a carpet of cushion mosses can be one of the most restful and uplifting sights in nature, softly covering the ground like drifts of snow.

If shade and acid soil are present, but there is little moisture, a moist situation can be introduced by installing a device that can be set to emit a cloud of mist over a designated area so moss can thrive even during dry periods. Also, it may be possible to encourage moss to grow on rotting wood placed across a running stream and on moist boulders that have their bases immersed in the stream.

One way to turn a neutral, slightly acid or alkaline soil into one that is acidic enough for moss to thrive, is to lay down plenty of well-decomposed organic matter, especially leaf mold, and to add garden sulphur to the indigenous soil. To introduce moss to a site, acquire squares of moss from a garden that already has plenty.

Moss does not look as attractive on a flat level surface as a shade-loving lawn grass which can be cut to a uniform height, but when the moss is allowed to grow over mounded and contoured ground, the hillocks create beautiful shadow patterns among the velvet-like texture of the moss. Moss should never be mowed, but whenever a brown patch appears and weeds start to sprout, eliminate them before they have a chance to gain a stranglehold, and patch the bare spot with new moss.

1

2

3

8

7

6

4

5

1 *Stone, moss and evergreen euonymus.* 2 *Slipper orchids in moss.* 3 *Japanese-style moss garden, Dans la Forêt, Pennsylvania.* 4 *Moss garden at Swiss Pines Japanese garden, Pennsylvania.* 5 *Moss garden with rustic gazebo, Dans la Forêt, Pennsylvania.* 6 *Mossy cliff with waterfalls.* 7 *Moss and ivy-covered tree trunk.* 8 *Moss-covered sheep shelter, Cutalossa Farm, Pennsylvania.*

Mounds, islands and pyramids

1
2

MOUNDS, ISLANDS AND PYRAMIDS Mounds often occur naturally in gardens, and they make good places to place a gazebo, bench, statue – or even a hot tub. Flat, level spaces often benefit from an artificial mound for a number of reasons – to provide an elevated view, to improve the appearance of a flat site, to create a focal point along a path, or to make an island in a pond. A mound that is used as an elevated viewpoint can also serve as a cellar for keeping wine cool and storing root crops through winter.

Mounds are usually circular to create a dome, but they can be any geometric shape. A moss-covered, pyramid-shaped mound features in the middle of a pond as a focal point in the Delaware garden of landscape designer Bill Frederick. A rectangular mound, covered in English ivy and a grove of trees, and accessible by a stairway, overlooks the maze of the Governor's Palace, Colonial Williamsburg.

Islands make ponds and lakes more interesting. The Japanese especially are masters at creating artificial islands, using boulders and contorted pines to create a beautiful accent. Islands can be completely surrounded by water, accessible only by boat, to make sanctuaries for waterfowl, like swans, to nest in peace. Islands can also be connected by stepping stones and bridges.

Pyramids introduce a mystical aura into a garden. They are normally built of stone and are best sited at the end of a vista as a dominant focal point, or at the end of an avenue of trees. They can function as a rain shelter, bath-house, tool-shed or toilet.

3

4

1 Man-made island with pruned weeping willows. 2 Mound topped by a raised stone hot tub. 3 Pond with moss-covered pyramid mound. 4 Stone cairn, The Garden House, UK. 5 Pyramid tool-shed, Château de Vendoeuvre, France.

5

Orchards and vineyards

ORCHARDS AND VINEYARDS Lucky indeed is the garden owner with space for a small orchard or vineyard, though the growing of most orchard fruits and grapes can be labor-intensive if heavy yields and blemish-free fruits are desired. Fruit trees can still be grown in limited space, by training them against walls and fences in espalier fashion (see page 72), and by growing special dwarf varieties, sometimes in roomy containers. Plant breeders have recently developed special fastigiate varieties of apples and pears, called 'Colonnade' fruit trees. These trees grow tall and narrow, ideal for planting along a sunny house foundation.

Vineyards on a large scale – covering a hundred acres or more – offer beautiful panoramic views, especially when the vine supports follow the contours of the land.

In the modest garden, to save space, grape vines are easily trained against walls and over trellis. A vineyard in Renoir's garden, near Nice, consists of a short fence rail at the edge of a terrace and room for the planting of three dessert-grape varieties – a white, red and black. Grape vines can be planted in whisky half-barrels to bear worthwhile yeilds.

1

3

2

1 *Small vineyard, Pennsbury Manor, Pennsylvania.* 2 *Roses and orange trees.* 3 *Dwarf potted apples.* 4 *Dwarf pear, Villandry, France.* 5 *Cordon fruit trees, Colonial Williamsburg.*

5

Orchid gardens

ORCHID GARDENS are mostly associated with tropical climates and conservatories, since the most exotic cannot tolerate frost. However, there are at least 15,000 species of orchid in the wild – distantly related to irises – and perhaps twice that number of hybrids. There are myriad reasons why orchids are so fascinating to study and collect. Many have near-human characteristics, with personalities and 'faces' formed by their distinctive flower shape and petal markings. In the wild, orchids can be terrestrial (ground dwelling) or epiphytic (tree dwelling). Although the most exotic orchids are tender to frost, and must be grown under glass, such as a conservatory or atrium, orchid enthusiasts can create the atmosphere of a tropical rainforest indoors even in a small setting, and during frost-free months move the collection to a special shaded outdoor area, such as a lathe house or a courtyard. The largest indoor orchid garden is located in the Durban Botanical Garden, South Africa, featuring hundreds of species growing around rock pools and waterfalls.

The five most popular orchid families are *Cattleya* (florist orchids), *Paphiopedilum* (slipper orchids), *Phalaenopsis* (moth orchids), *Miltonia* (pansy orchids), *Cymbidium* (mountain orchids) and *Oncidium* (dancing lady orchids). Among hardy orchids, consider the pink lady's slipper orchid (*Cypripedium acaule*), also *Pleione* and two kinds of marsh orchid – *Dactylorhiza foliosa*, which prefers gritty, well drained soil, and *Dactylorhiza maculata*, which will colonize boggy meadows.

1

2

3

4

5

1 *Orchid garden, Durban Botanical Garden.* 2 *Orchid house, Cedaridge Farm.* 3 *Marsh orchid meadow, Shetland.* 4 Pleione *orchids and cycad.* 5 Cymbidium *orchids, coastal garden.*

Parterres

PARTERRES consist of low hedges that help define a pattern. The garden spaces within that pattern can be filled either with colored gravel, flowering plants or herbs. Parterres are frequently found in company with topiary gardens, the parterres creating interest at ground level, and the topiary taking it to eye height and above. The preferred plant for parterres is hardy evergreen boxwood because it is slow growing and its dense knit of dark green branches and leaves is easily pruned, but other choices include silvery lavender cotton, golden dwarf berberis, bronze dwarf berberis, blue squamata juniper and rich green box honeysuckle (*Lonicera nitida*). These can be planted to form ribbons so the colors intertwine, creating what is commonly called a knot garden (see page 111).

1

1 *Château de Sassy, France.* **2** *Château de Villandry, France.*

2

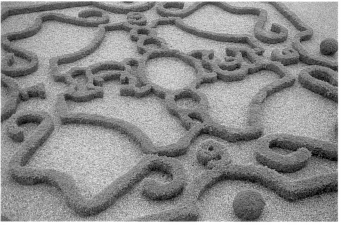

1

2

The most extensive and intricate parterre designs exist in France and Scotland, particularly at Versailles Palace, near Paris, Villandry in the Loire valley, and Drummond Castle, Perthshire. Much smaller examples of parterre designs can be seen in the historic areas of Charleston, South Carolina, and Colonial Williamsburg, Virginia.

Parterre de broderie is a style of French parterre design featuring an embroidery-like pattern of flourishes and scrolls.

1 *All-white garden with gray lavender-cotton parterre.*
2 *Embroidery-style parterre.* 3 *Boxwood parterre.*

3

Paths

PATHS help visitors explore a garden, and their placement should be decided in the early stages of a design, for paths help to establish the bones more than any other consideration. Claude Monet's garden, for example, uses two styles of path to accomplish two distinctly different types of effect. In the Clos Normand, a flower garden extending from Monet's house to the bottom of the property, paths are straight and narrow, creating long lines of perspective. In the early spring before flowers fill in the edges and blur the straight lines, the paths are formal, called plant bands and their purpose is to give the garden a sense of greater depth. Indeed, on rainy days and misty mornings the paths seem to lead off into infinity. Yet viewed from right angles, the paths are hidden and the design no longer looks formal because the plants all seem to merge like waves of surf, creating the appearance of a seamless meadow garden.

Crossing the road at the bottom of Monet's flower garden, visitors enter another world altogether. This is Monet's water garden, with a meandering path that has no straight lines. It simply follows the curvature of the pond, creating a visual adventure as it completes a circuit that leads from one observation point to another. The focus of this garden is invariably the water reflections and the pond surface with its islands of waterlilies. It is a path for strolling, leading from a high-arched bridge at the start of the journey, through groves of bamboo, beneath arches of roses, to a smaller, low-arched bridge, under the waving branches of weeping willow. Everywhere the walk encourages introspection, the eye always drawn to the center of the pond. A common denominator is the gravel path, composed of the same beige-colored pea gravel.

In gardens, a path can take the shortest route from one destination to another, particularly in highly formal gardens where straight lines are desirable, or it can take the

1

4

3

2

1 *Brick path and grasses.* 2 *Japanese-style path.* 3 *Brick path beside exposed tree roots.* 4 *Crazy-paving path.*

1

longest route, meandering back and forth in hairpin turns. On a flat plane the meandering path can present a wealth of visual delights in a relatively small space, but when a path is screened too much it can create a sinister, claustrophobic aura. Variations in the walking surface can help break up the monotony. In a larger garden, a path's surface material could begin with gravel, change to flagstone, then cobblestone, then wood chips or pine needles. Even wooden slabs can be used for paving, the slabs and stones laid out in different patterns for eye appeal.

The paving material for paths must be firmly seated if it is substantial, like bricks, Belgian blocks or flagstone. To prevent slippage during storms, or wobbling during heavy traffic, paving of this type should be laid on a bed of crushed stones or sand, depending on the firmness of the indigenous soil. Less durable paving like pine needles, licorice root, shredded pine bark and wood chips should be laid between a raised edging to reduce the chance of it being blown away by wind. Heavy rains can also play havoc with these perishable

8

2

3

4

5

6

7

materials, and so runnels may be needed to divert water away from a path.

On a steep hillside paths can zig-zag for comfort, making the descent an easy walk, and allowing the visitor to look out at a scenic panorama if the view is not obscured by structures or vegetation. If paths lead downhill at too sharp an incline they can become dangerous, especially when wet or icy, and so if a steep descent is desirable (for example to create an axis or a shortcut), then it may be best to install a flight of steps between terraced sections of the path.

Grass paths are restful to look at, but should be avoided on slopes because they become exceedingly slippery when wet, even from a slight coating of morning dew. Grass paths are good to consider for dividing sunny, level parallel borders because most turf grasses grow best in full sun. For grass paths through woodland, choose a shade-tolerant variety like fine fescue. It may also help to prune trees of all lower branches so filtered light ensures strong green grass growth.

Paths help orchestrate movement through a garden. A narrow, straight path will hurry people along, while a broad path will encourage visitors to slow down and amble. To deceive the eye into extending distance, a path can start wide, and in stages become narrower, so the length appears greater than it really is.

Good drainage is essential for all paths so that they do not puddle water after rain. Where paths lead through boggy areas it may be necessary to create a raised causeway of stones, and even a boardwalk.

1 and 6 Same gravel footpath in autumn and spring. 2 Gravel woodland path, Monet's garden. 3 Petals carpeting gravel path, Bodnant, UK. 4 Woodland path. 5 Gravel path in Monet's garden. 7 Belgian block path. 8 Japanese-style cobblestone path.

The simplest paths to make consist of gravel, shell or woodchips. Often, all that's needed is to mow the pathway, treat the growth with a weedkiller to remove the indigenous vegetation along its course, and then lay your chosen material directly in place. To traverse a meadow, a surface material may not be necessary at all. Simply take a mower and cut your path through it. At Cedaridge Farm a straight wide path up a sloping meadow leads from the farmhouse to a distant grove of trees. The closely-cropped grass defines the path and creates a beautiful vista. A path is mowed along the outer edges of the meadow as well to create a nature trail which visitors can also use for jogging.

All things considered, it is most often the paths through gardens that make a visit memorable, for even in neglected gardens, a well-defined path can help produce an exciting experience. Though Monet's garden is manicured, Cezanne's restored garden looks neglected because he wanted to see nature always reclaiming man's dominion. Both artists used a device that is fleeting in its effect, but especially appealing in a naturalistic setting – the idea of planting flowering trees over a path deliberately to allow the petals to drop and color the path. Both used blue wisteria blossoms and the rosy-red petals of Judas trees to color the ground, though ornamental cherries, rhododendrons and camellias are also good choices. The effect may last only a day or two before the spent petals shrivel and dry, but that pool of color along a winding path can be an uplifting sight.

1 *Asphalt path carpeted with camellia petals.* 2 *Beach-front path.* 3 *Grassy woodland path, Cedaridge Farm.*

Paving

PAVING The blocky cobblestone paving patterns of Belgian thoroughfares, the pebble path mosaics of Islamic gardens, the terracotta tilework of Spanish courtyards, the flagstones of Italian terraces, the broken stone slabs of Japanese temple forecourts – all have had an influence on modern garden design where a durable, hard surface is needed to keep feet dry and make walking comfortable.

Paving reduces maintenance, whether used to make a path, create a terrace or establish the floor of a courtyard. Because of its flatness, it is the hardscape element that can contrast most pleasantly with plants. Though paving reduces the planting area, it can create strong bones for a garden – like walls – and it aids the designer in deciding what plants to select – perhaps a low edging of box as a transitional element between the paving and flower beds.

Paving cannot compete with a lawn for restfulness on the eye, but hard paving can be beautiful in the patterns and colors of the material used. Paving also reflects light in different ways. A light-colored paving can improve growth of plants in a shaded area, a dark paving reduce glare in a sunny area.

In addition to a number of natural paving materials, including flagstone, thick slate, cobblestones, and wooden pavers, there are manufactured materials, especially concrete, tile and brick.

With concrete there are many ways to create a textured surface so the utilitarian look of the paving is disguised. One way is to press into the surface smooth round pebbles, small mosaic tiles, and even pieces of colored glass. Coloring agents can also be applied to reduce glare and the monotony of concrete slabs. With brick, there are countless ways to create a distinctive pattern, for example bricks laid in herringbone and checkerboard styles. Flagstone is the most durable paving material, available in uniform sizes for formal gardens and random sizes for a more natural, rustic look. Tile paving is associated with Spanish and Moorish gardens. Though handmade tiles are expensive, they can produce a distinctive, sophisticated look, especially for historic properties. Machine-made tiles are available in myriad designs, some deliberately made to look used.

Wood paving is generally produced from using landscape ties, available from lumber yards, or wood rounds which are produced from sawing a tree trunk across the grain in uniform slices. These can be treated to make them rot resistant.

1

2

4

3

1 *Patio of flagstone pavers.* **2** *Patio of brick paving.* **3** *Stepping stone brick pavers.* **4** *Crazy paving.*

Perennial gardens

PERENNIAL GARDENS are composed of plants that can stay in place from year to year, their clumps of foliage and flowering display sometimes doubling in size each season, and they are often reasonably carefree. Some of the most easy-care have a short flowering season – peonies, bearded irises, garden lilies, daylilies and oriental poppies, for example – but they are hardy and produce such a big impact when they are in bloom, it is advisable to plan mixed beds and borders around them. It is wise to make sure there is something coming into bloom before and after these 'big five' command the scene.

In addition to perennials that provide a fleeting moment of floral impact, there is a small group of hardy perennials that bloom non-stop for most of the summer season. These include the hardy hibiscus *H. moscheutos* in pink, red and white, the miniature orange daylily 'Stella d'Oro', sage 'Lady-in-Red', and pink and white *Gaura lindheimeri*.

Most important for continuous color are perennials noted for long-lasting foliage. The hardy hostas 'Blue Angel' and 'Sum-and-Substance' (a chartreuse) not only have colorful leaves but also produce spires of white or pale lilac tubular flowers into the bargain. Both are good for planting in light shade and moist soil. Remember, too, that ferns are perennial and make a good contrast with hostas in shady areas. Most grasses are also perennial, and though the majority prefer full sun, there are shade-tolerant kinds like Bowles' golden sedge and Japanese woodland grass.

Even if you desire a perennial planting with color orchestrated to occur throughout the flowering season, it's best to decide a peak flowering period, then spread the color for the rest of the season with supporting players. A shady perennial garden might be planted to produce its strongest color impact in early spring, when an extremely large number of shade-loving plants bloom, including columbine, hellebore, primula, trillium, Jacob's ladder, blue woodland phlox, and dame's rocket. However, for a sensational color burst in full sun, it might be better to plan for peak color in mid-summer, using scene-stealers such as perennial sunflowers (*Heliopsis helianthoides*), sneezeweed (*Helenium autumnale*), stonecrop sedum, Joe Pye weed (*Eupatorium purpureum*), astilbe, shasta daisies, poker plants and bee balm (*Monarda didyma*).

A deep, fertile soil and good drainage is essential for most perennial plants, especially when considering a mixed perennial border. Where foraging animals such as rabbits and deer are a nuisance, it may be advisable to protect perennial plantings with a liquid repellent sprayed onto foliage.

After three years, consider digging up established clumps of perennials and dividing them. Plants like yarrow and rudbeckia can make such thick, spreading root masses they become invasive and crowd out less vigorous plants like lilies.

The most popular perennial garden design is the sunny perennial border backed by a hedge, fence or wall. A refinement is the double perennial border where parallel beds are separated by a grass, brick or flagstone walk. One of the largest

1

6

7

2

3

5

1 *Olive Dunn's cottage garden, New Zealand.* **2** *Barnhaven primroses, Cedaridge Farm.* **3** *Late summer perennial border.* **4** *Perennial island bed.* **5** *Candelabra verbascum and fleabane.* **6** *Lakeside perennials, ligularia 'Othello' and astilbe.* **7** *Double perennial border.*

4

1

2

3

8

double perennial borders in Europe is at the Royal Horticultural Society headquarters, Wisley, where a perennial planting known as the Oudolf Borders, for their designer Piet Oudolf, extend down a slope from the Fruit Mount to a conservatory complex, the mount itself providing a high elevated view to fully appreciate the extent of the awesome design.

At Bressingham Gardens, Norfolk, Adrian Bloom showed the world how to make perennial plantings appealing by planting them as island beds around a bowl-shaped depression called The Dell, where a thatched stone gazebo stands in the center, and weeping willows extend their curtains of slender leaves high into the sky.

Monet considered his garden at its peak during the first week of June when multi-colored perennial bearded irises, pink peonies, blood-red Oriental poppies and pink roses trained on trellis, all bloomed together. Later in the season, long brushstrokes of yellow perennial sunflowers bloom

4

5

6

behind lower growing blue New England asters to create a yellow-and-blue color harmony on opposite sides of the Grande Allée. Although Asiatic hybrid garden lilies are the scene stealers in mid-summer, that is also when Monet's collection of perennial waterlilies reach peak bloom to create a highlight in his water garden.

In the USA, at Unionville, Pennsylvania, Sir John Thouron has implemented one of the world's largest sunny perennial gardens at his home, Doe Run. The biggest bed is undulating and extends along a lawn vista that seems to disappear into infinity: its large drifts of perennials are orchestrated to reach peak bloom in July.

In addition to perennials for mixed borders in sunny, dry places such as rock gardens (see page 151), and shade-loving perennials for woodland, many varieties are suitable for other site-specific locations such as boggy soil (see page 37). Instead of mixing perennials in a bog garden, especially where space is limited, it might be more desirable to establish a large colony of a particular variety; for example, a mass of candelabra primulas or Japanese water iris.

1 Annual red orache veils perennial pink Joe-pye weed.
2 Bearded irises, Cedaridge Farm. 3 Double perennial border, Parkside garden, New Zealand. 4 Miniature daffodils and hellebores, Cedaridge Farm. 5 Hostas in shade. 6 Double perennial borders, Larnach Castle, New Zealand. 7 English perennial border, Bodnant, Wales. 8 Wedding garden, Parkside, New Zealand.

7

Pergolas

PERGOLAS are passageways that can connect an outbuilding to the main house or connect two parts of a garden. They are usually composed of substantial pillars made from wooden posts, stone or brick, topped by an open framework of beams to support heavy vines. A stroll beneath a flowering pergola can be a romantic experience, and at Hearst Castle, California, a pergola was built sufficiently wide and high for a pair of horse riders to move through unimpeded.

Pergolas feature prominently in Italian Renaissance gardens and were used predominantly to follow the curve of a hillside. British Victorian-era architect Sir Edwin Lutyens built pergolas of brick, allowing him to echo the strong architectural lines of his brick residences. A particularly fine example of his work can be seen today in France at Parc Floral des Moutiers, near Dieppe, where a straight pergola leads visitors to a rose garden. La Mortola, a splendid restored Italian coastal garden at Ventimiglia, on the Italian/French border, features a broad curved pergola smothered by tender flowering vines and underplanted with clivia. Windows cut into the foliage provide exceptional views of the valley garden and the sea below.

Suitable vines for covering pergolas include wisteria, climbing roses, clematis, trumpet creeper and grapes.

1

2

4

3

1 Pergola, Longwood Gardens, Pennsylvania. 2 Pergola, Burle-Marx design, Auckland. 3 Pergola, Wave Hill garden, New York. 4 Pergola, Sir Edwin Lutyens design, Parc Floral des Moutiers, France.

Playhouses and tree-houses

PLAYHOUSES AND TREE-HOUSES are fun places for children and the young in heart. One of the most ambitious playhouses was constructed for Marie Antoinette to entertain herself and courtiers. When she wanted to escape the strictures and formality of court life at Versailles Palace, she retired to Le Petit Hameau, a community of quaint cottages and a mill grouped around a small lake covered in waterlilies.

Playhouses usually consist of a small building for children, sometimes imitating a familiar structure from the world of children's novels, such as a gingerbread house, a Swiss chalet, a giant mushroom and even an old shoe. They can be miniature cottages resembling dolls' houses, and filled with child-size furniture.

Tree-houses can also serve as playhouses, or they can be more practical structures intended to provide an elevated view. In Kruger National Park, South Africa, a tree-house built in a ranger's garden provides a clear view over the perimeter fence to a watering-hole where lions, giraffes, zebras and elephants often drink. An unusually large tree-house existed for years in a giant kapok tree at the Victoria Hotel, Nassau, in the Bahamas. Several platforms were featured: one level supported a dance floor and dining tables, another level a bar, while a third level accommodated an entire orchestra. It was an especially popular place in the evening, its branches strung with lights.

1 *Playhouse, Larnach Castle, New Zealand.* 2 *Playhouse, Winterthur, Delaware.* 3 *Tree house, Cezanne's Garden, France.* 4 *Playhouse, Savannah suburban garden, Georgia.* 5 *Redwood tree house, Salinas garden, California.*

1

2

3

5

4

Pleaching and pollarding

1

PLEACHING AND POLLARDING are different forms of pruning to create special effects with trees. Pleaching is the pruning and shaping of trees so that they can be woven or trained over a temporary frame to create a self-sustaining tunnel, or to make a formal aerial hedge, the top growth of foliage supported by column-like trunks devoid of lower side branches. Pleaching can also create elaborate arches, and hedges to resemble walls with windows cut into them. Pleaching differs from topiary in that the pruning is architectural in appearance, while topiary forms tend to be free-standing representations of people and animals, and more whimsical.

Pleaching is a favorite feature of French and Italian formal gardens, and indeed, in many parts of France, such as at Vernon, Normandy, pleached aerial hedges of lime trees extend for miles from the edge of town into the countryside to create a pleached allée.

At Dumbarton Oaks, Washington DC, an aerial hedge forms an ellipse, with an ornate fountain in the middle. The trees are American hornbeam, which resemble beech trees, a favorite choice for pleaching in Europe. At the Ladew Topiary Gardens, Maryland, sections of pleached hedges encircle an oval lawn called The Grand Bowl, the walls of greenery pierced by openings, the top pruned to form garlands. There are doors

1 Pleached linden avenue, Vernon, France. 2 Pleached beech hedge, Heronswood, Washington State. 3 Pollarded willow, Monet's garden. 4 Pleached beech alley. 5 Pleached hemlock hedge in snow, Ladew Topiary Gardens, Maryland.

2

3

4

and windows of hemlock, and the entire spectacle never looks lovelier than on a winter's day when a light dusting of snow accentuates the architectural lines.

The pleached alleys of France or the pleached hedges of the Ladew Topiary Gardens are not easy to incorporate into small properties, but at Heronswood, Washington State, a short span of pleached arches adds distinction to a small garden. The Ghost Walk, at Old Westbury Gardens, New York State, is also an example of pleaching that can fit into a small garden. The Ghost Walk is simply a path separated by yew hedges where the top branches have been arched upward and inward to form a dark, eerie tunnel of sinuous branches. A peacock sculpture in an oasis of light at the end makes an appropriate focal point.

Pollarding is the cutting back of branches to the crown of a tree so it shoots out new juvenile growth. This can be an important maintenance chore with aerial pleached alleys in order to keep the hedge effect tidy. However, pollarding is mostly done on willows to make them sprout an explosion of branches at all angles. When it is done with willows that have colorful bark, such as golden willows, the effect can be extremely decorative.

5

Ponds

PONDS are pools of water intended to attract wildlife or accommodate a collection of fish, such as koi and goldfish, or accommodate a collection of water plants such as waterlilies and lotus. Ponds are normally irregular in shape, the edges softened with ferns and water plants such as flag irises, cardinal flowers (*Lobelia cardinalis*) and cat-tails (*Typha*), and they are generally much less maintenance than an ornamental pool, with its working parts, such as filters and pumps.

At Cedaridge Farm there are two ponds; one made by damming a small stream to back up the water, the other an artificial pond made by scooping out a depression and making it waterproof with an impervious liner. The building of even a small pond can be a tricky undertaking and so it is best to consult with professionals experienced in their installation, particularly on the question of depth needed to keep fish healthy, the choice of liner (for example natural clay verses a flexible membrane), the number of oxygenating plants needed to keep the water healthy without a filter system, and even the proper placement of the pond, since the lowest level on the property may not be an ideal site. Be aware, also, that the disturbance of existing wetland areas may require a permit.

1

2

1 *Woodland pond with log edging.* 2 *New Zealand flax and variegated iris light up a hillside pond.* 3 *Wildlife pond framed by 'Heritage' river birch, Cedaridge Farm.* 4 *Wildlife pond in autumn.*

4

3

1

2

3

This is particularly true if you plan to dam a stream in order to create the pond.

Ponds are best located in a sunny position for the health of fish. If trees, such as river birch with their decorative bark, and weeping willows with their curtains of leaves swaying in the breeze, are desired alongside the pond, these should be concentrated on the north side and set back from its banks if possible.

Monet's famous pond, with its collection of waterlilies and exquisite water reflections, was created in a swampy area by diverting water from a small stream and using sluice gates to regulate the flow in and out of the pond.

1 *Waterlily pond, Attadale garden, Scotland.* 2 *Lotus pond, Chanticleer garden, Pennsylvania.* 3 *Wildlife pond, Aegis House, Scotland.* 4 *Pool with goldfish, Bellevue garden, New Zealand.*

4

Porches and verandas

PORCHES AND VERANDAS are mostly wooden decks attached to a house, roofed to provide shelter, for sitting and entertaining outdoors. Porches usually extend across the front of the house, on either side of the entrance, while verandas (from the Hindu word, *varanda*) will often wrap around, and even completely surround a residence. Both are a common feature of pioneer housing, particularly colonial homes where they became a favorite place to sit during hot summers, fitted with swing benches to relax. They are also good places to decorate with hanging baskets or groups of potted plants. In areas with biting insects, both porches and verandas can be screened.

A very fine veranda surrounds the main house at Magnolia Plantation, South Carolina, for it is wide enough to entertain large groups. By wrapping around the house completely, it provides spectacular views on four sides – two sides being elevated above adjacent woodland, while that at the front overlooks the entrance driveway lined with live oak trees draped in Spanish moss. From the rear one enjoys a lawn vista to the Ashley River.

1 *Veranda, Magnolia Plantation, South Carolina.*
2 *Porch, Hortensia garden, New Zealand.* 3 *Porch, Cutalossa Farm, Pennsylvania.* 4 *Veranda, Pennypack Mills, Pennsylvania.*

1

2

3

4

Raised beds

RAISED BEDS can be both decorative and functional structures in the landscape. Functionally, they allow for plants to be grown on difficult soil, such as stony, boggy or impoverished earth. The height of the new growing medium above the indigenous soil should be at least 12 inches for annuals and perennials, more for trees and shrubs, depending on size. To get the most soil depth from a raised bed, consider digging up the indigenous soil and improving it with compost before introducing screened garden topsoil for the growing area. Where a site has poor drainage, lay down a bed of crushed stones beneath the screened topsoil.

Ideal materials for creating raised beds include stones, brick, wooden planks, landscape ties, and even wattle. Vegetable growers find raised beds are ideal for salad greens and herbs. They are equally desirable for growing root crops such as carrots and parsnips since a special sandy soil mix can be formulated to allow the roots to penetrate deep down without becoming distorted from stones, lumps of clay and debris. People with disabilities – such as those in wheelchairs – who find it difficult to cultivate a garden at soil level, often find it easier when beds are raised.

For ornamental effect, raised beds don't have to be square or rectangular. They can take any geometric shape, such as circular and kidney-shaped, and they can be set out in appealing patterns to create a parterre design.

1

8

7

2

3

5

4

6

1 *Enabling garden of raised beds, Longwood Gardens, Pennsylvania.* 2 *Salad greens and herbs.* 3 *Island beds of begonias, Butchard Gardens, Canada.* 4 *Raised beds for herbs using juniper trunks.* 5 *Space-saving terraced pyramid planter.* 6 *Circular driveway with raised island bed for pine tree.* 7 *Raised beds, Cedaridge Farm.* 8 *Wattle fencing, Priory d'Orsan, France.*

Reflections

REFLECTIONS can double the beauty of a garden, either through a reflective water surface or a reflective glass surface, like a mirror. It was Monet who recognized the special quality that reflections could add to his water garden so that in his later years his pond reflections became his favorite motif. He made his painting all the more mysterious by painting reflections with no horizon line between islands of waterlily foliage, so the waterlily flowers and leaves (called pads), would seem to be floating in air. Though Monet's pond was surrounded by trees that naturally cast reflections, with an opening to the sky that often was imbued with exquisite sunrise and sunset colors, he deliberately planted the edges of the pond to intensify its reflections, strategically placing a green, arching bridge so it would create an oval when mirrored in the water, and planting trellises festooned with rambler roses and wisteria so pink and blue would also feature in the reflections.

At the garden of Cobamong, New York, exquisite reflections occur in autumn when a large number of white birch around the rim of a lake have mirrored in the water their ghostly bark and golden leaves in company with other trees and shrubs noted for strong autumn colors, including Japanese maples, viburnum and oakleaf hydrangea.

One of the most desirable reflections to have in a garden is that of the moon, which may require a special elevated observation platform to be built so the moon can be seen in the very center of an expanse of water. The high arch of a bridge may also achieve the necessary elevation.

1 *Bridge reflection, Magnolia Plantation, South Carolina.*
2 *Lake-side reflection, Cobamong garden, New York State.*
3 *Morning reflection, Pine Mountain, Florida.* **4** *Pond reflection, Monet's garden.*

1

2

4

3

Rhododendron gardens

RHODODENDRON GARDENS There are certain plant families guaranteed to attract crowds. For example, tulips are the big draw at Keukenhof Gardens, Holland; irises take center stage at the Presby Iris Gardens, New Jersey; tree ferns draw hoards of visitors to the Lost Gardens of Heligan, Cornwall; flowering cherries are the main attraction of many of Japan's public gardens; moss draws thousands more to others. The Bagatelle Rose Gardens near Paris, and the Portland Rose Garden, Oregon, are world famous for their collections of both modern and old garden roses. However, it is the plant family known as rhododendron (which includes azaleas) on which the reputations of many gardens are built. This includes Britain's most admired garden, Bodnant, in North Wales; Parc Floral des Moutiers, on the Normandy coast; New Zealand's Pukeiti Rhododendron Garden, at New Plymouth; Cross Hills, at Kimbolton, also Glenfalloch and Maple Glen, in that country's South Island: plus many large woodland gardens in Scotland and the Pacific Northwest, where conditions for growing rhododendrons are ideal.

Botanically, there is no difference between a rhododendron and an azalea, for they are both members of the genus Rhododendron, but nurserymen and gardeners like to make a distinction on the basis of appearance, rhododendrons generally having larger leaves and larger flowers.

Azaleas can be sheared to keep them compact, but it is best not to prune a rhododendron because this means the loss of flowering ability for the following season, whereas azaleas, if sheared by mid-summer, can still have time to develop flower buds for bloom the following season. At Magnolia Plantation, South Carolina, it is the azalea-type rhododendrons known as *Rhododendron indica* that reign supreme, owing to their heat tolerance.

1 *Rhododendron 'Peter Allen', Carlson Garden, New York State.* **2** *Heritage Plantation, home of Dexter hybrid rhododendrons, Massachusetts.* **3** *Azalea slope with Cherokee rose, Middleton Place garden, South Carolina.* **4** *Bluebells and Exbury hybrid azaleas, Van Dusen garden, Canada.*

1 *Rhododendron 'Cynthia', Bois des Moutiers, France.* 2 *Ilam Homestead, New Zealand, home of Ilam hybrid rhododendrons.* 3 *Indica azaleas, Magnolia Plantation, South Carolina.* 4 *Rhododendron 'Scintillation'* and cabbage trees, New Zealand.

Azaleas can be divided into evergreen and deciduous. The famous Exbury strain of deciduous azalea is most desired for its orange and yellow shades and strong fragrance, though the plants tend to be short-lived where summers are hot.

A bush of rhododendron can grow to 80 feet in height, covered in so many blooms – up to the size of soccer balls – they almost hide the foliage. They grow well in sun or light shade, can be planted to line driveways, create thickets, form hedges and make good companions with camellias, but generally they demand sharp drainage and acid soil. Where natural rainfall is sparse in summer, they may need irrigation.

Lionel de Rothschild created one of the most beautiful rhododendron gardens in Britain at Exbury, near Southampton, where he planted the best rhododendrons from his hybridizing program, using wild species collected from the Himalayas and North America. By the time he died in 1942 he had raised more than 500 varieties as a result of instinctively knowing the probable outcome of crossing two selected parents. On at least one occasion he sent his chauffeur hundreds of miles into Scotland to collect pollen from a particularly vigorous, free-flowering specimen he thought would make a superior male parent.

One of North America's leading rhododendron breeders, Joseph Gable, was propelled from relative obscurity to overnight fame by an article in a leading magazine with the headline 'The Flaming Forest of Joe Gable' and photographs of his Pennsylvania farm brilliant with the blossoms of azaleas planted in woodland.

In New Zealand an aggressive hybridizing program by Edgar Stead (1877–1949), at Ilam Homestead, Christchurch, resulted in drought-tolerant rhododendron varieties known as the Ilam hybrids. Today, the garden Stead planted around the homestead, now part of the Canterbury University campus, is occasionally open to the public. Once one of the most beautiful in New Zealand, it features three romantic Monet-style bridges and woodland paths that are most colorful in late October.

Rock gardens

ROCK GARDENS have been described as the 'most amount of work for the least amount of satisfaction' because of the constant maintenance an attractive rock garden generally needs, with its diminutive cushions of alpine plants constantly threatened with destruction from aggressive weed growth. But that type of rock garden – a space that emulates an alpine scree or rock fall – is rarely seen in home gardens, and more often made under the protection of glass in a special alpine house. The type of rock garden popular in home gardens today will likely feature a waterfall or pool as its central decorative element, and display a lot of easy-care plants like dwarf evergreen Alberta spruce, mugo pines, 'Blue Rug' junipers, and tough, spreading flowering groundcovers like blue bugle (*Ajuga*) and creeping jenny (*Lysimachia*), with the ability to crowd out weeds.

Though rock gardens can be made on flat ground, they are best displayed on slopes, with natural flat areas interspersed among outcrops of boulders to form rocky terraces. A common mistake is to choose boulders no bigger than a single person can lift. This leads to monotony. The cost of paying for a contractor to bring in equipment for moving extra-heavy boulders is generally well worth it.

1 *Glencoe Farm rock garden, Pennsylvania.* 2 *Japanese-style rock garden.* 3 *Chisaku-in temple garden, Kyoto.* 4 *Rock garden, Dunedin Botanical Garden.*

1

2

3

Rock gardens can be established to help create a theme. In addition to surrounding a water garden, for example, they can be designed to harbor a special plant collection, such as ferns and orchids. Using predominantly dwarf evergreens, they can help evoke a Japanese garden.

One of the world's largest rock gardens is located on a sunny slope beside the Leith Stream in the Dunedin Botanical Garden, New Zealand. Covering over 2000 square yards, this took seven years to build and features basalt rocks from nearby Mount Cargill for its solid outcrops. Pockets of soil are here planted with drifts of rock jasmine, hardy geranium and sea pinks among clumps of silvery native Marlborough rock daisies (*Olearia insignis*), golden speargrass (*Aciphylla squarrosa*), moss-like vegetable sheep (*Raoulia bryoides*) and spires of dwarf conifers.

1 *Rock garden, Cedaridge Farm.* 2 *Orchid* Dactylorizha foliosa, *Reginald Kaye rock garden, UK.* 3 *Rock garden at Innisfree, New York State.* 4 *Tony Schillig's rock garden, Scotland.*

4

Rooftop gardens

ROOFTOP GARDENS are generally associated with cities, allowing apartment owners to cultivate a garden in a soil-less environment. Normally, a flat, impervious surface must serve as a base for wooden decking to support containers with watering trays. Renters invariably must obtain a landlord's permission, since any overload on a roof can have disastrous consequences, such as leakage from excessive watering, and even collapse if too heavy a soil load is applied.

Because space is usually at a premium, a rooftop garden must be designed so that plants grow up rather than spread out, and, therefore, for decorative effect it's good to consider tall wind-resistant spire-like plants such as hollyhock, and vines like nasturtiums and morning glories. If vegetables are desired, then pole beans and other vine crops like tomatoes and cucumbers can be staked to grow upwards.

The best rooftop gardens will feature a shaded sitting-out area and small greenhouse, or the rooftop will be accessible through a conservatory so that exotic species like banana trees and tree ferns can be moved outdoors during frost-free months.

1

1 *Rooftop gardens, Eze, France.* 2 *Roof planted with succulents, Big Sur, California.* 3 *Roof garden, Philadelphia, USA.* 4 and 5 *Drozd rooftop garden, Philadelphia, Pennsylvania.*

2

4

3

5

Rose gardens

ROSE GARDENS can be formal and informal, and though the tendency is to display roses in borders, or in beds forming a grid pattern, the range of growth habits allows roses to be used informally with other plants. Perhaps no gardener integrated roses into a garden setting more successfully than Claude Monet. In his Clos Normand flower garden, roses are used in every conceivable way – climbers and ramblers to carry color high into the sky, even to cover high arches; shrub roses trained into standards or tree forms, a topknot of bloom resplendent on a slim woody trunk; old garden roses trained to create a pillar of bloom entwined with flowering clematis of a contrasting color; spreading roses like 'The Fairy' and 'Nevada' planted beside a pond so their canes arch out over water to create a waterfall of blossoms; miniature roses displayed in pots; and traditional floribundas and hybrid teas as specimens in beds and borders. Monet's garden also features lots of roses in company with tall perennials, such as Asiatic lilies and blue delphinium.

When creating a garden space exclusively for roses, it's good to choose a sunny position, and soil with good drainage. Though roses can be afflicted with a multitude of diseases, such as mildew and black spot, most can be controlled by sprays and there are disease-resistant varieties. The flowering of 'perpetual-blooming' or 'repeat blooming' varieties is largely dependent on the soil remaining cool. In areas with hot, humid summers, the soil can be kept cool by mulching the beds with gravel.

In recent years gardeners have developed a fondness for old garden roses to such an extent that modern hybrid teas and floribundas are often excluded, in preference to varieties with sweet-smelling, swirling petal patterns or varieties developed with an old-fashioned appearance, like those from British rosarian David Austin.

The famous rose garden in the Bagatelle Park of the Bois de Boulogne, Paris, was established in 1906, and remains one of France's premier rose gardens, featuring roses displayed in many ways, even as pillars and hedges. Each year Bagatelle sponsors a contest to make awards of recognition for the best new roses. It was during the judging one year that Claude Monet discovered what was to become one of his favorite roses, a climber named 'American Pillar', submitted by rosarian Conard Pyle from Pennsylvania. Monet persuaded the head gardener to provide him with some cuttings, and propagated it to climb over high arches above his boat dock in the water garden. The artist also gave away potted plants of his rose to friends.

Another spectacular French rose garden is the Roseraie de l'Hay, near Paris, where thousands of roses are trained high on arches and up vast sections of trellis. In France, the premier rose breeder is Meilland, responsible for the remarkably free-flowering family of shrub roses known as 'Meidiland', of which 'Bonica' and 'Red Meidiland' are highly disease-resistant.

1

7

6

Both Great Britain and New Zealand have superb climates for growing roses. The Irish rosarian, Dr Sam McGredy, found New Zealand so advantageous that in 1972 he moved his breeding program there from his homeland. He went on to produce some of the most free-flowering roses the world has ever seen, including his best selling 'Sexy Rexy'. In New Zealand, Auckland's Parnell Rose Gardens, the Hamilton Rose Gardens and the Wellington Rose Gardens are good places in the North Island to view McGredy's work in beds that feature both old and modern roses. In the South Island the cities of Christchurch, Dunedin and Invercargill also feature world-class rose gardens.

In Britain, the display garden of rosarian David Austin at Albrighton is considered among the most beautiful in Europe. The five individual gardens are formal, all sheltered by clipped conifer hedges, with the beds and borders edged in box or yew. Examples of Mrs. Pat Austin's sculpture are used as focal points.

The Portland International Rose Garden, overlooking the city in Oregon, is the most comprehensive rose garden in the USA, featuring a test garden with beds and borders of old and modern roses planted on slopes and terraces.

1 'Meidiland Scarlet' *shrub rose, Cedaridge Farm.* 2 *Hotel Baudy garden of old roses, Giverny, France.* 3 *Portland International Rose Garden, Oregon.* 4 *Hotel Baudy garden of old roses, Giverny, France.* 5 *Cottage garden filled with climbing and miniature roses.* 6 *Formal rose garden, Van Dusen Garden, Canada.* 7 *Bagatelle Rose Garden, Paris.*

Ruins, towers and follies

RUINS, TOWERS AND FOLLIES invite exploration, but according to William Gilpin, writing in 1772, 'It is not every man who can build a house who can execute a ruin.' To give the stone its look of antiquity, to place scattered heaps of ruin with an appearance of neglect, requires an artistic appreciation 'much too delicate for the hand of a common workman, and what we rarely see performed,' Gilpin concluded.

Ruins arc an unexpected embellishment to a garden, giving it a sense of antiquity, romance and mystery. The Impressionist painter Paul Cezanne found it comforting to discover ruins in the landscape, and the sight of nature reclaiming man's dominion was a recurring theme in his paintings, which frequently depicted ruins cloaked in ivy or framed by the twisted, sinuous branches of mature shrubs and trees.

Not all gardens have the space or design integrity for a ruin, but even a small garden can generally find room for part of a ruined wall to accommodate a collection of, for instance, tree peonies, which seem to like old stonework for company.

Where a garden lacks a ready-made ruin, one can be constructed. At The Garden House, Buckland Monochorum, in Devon, there is a beautiful genuine ruined tower – all that remains of a former abbot's house which fell into disrepair after the dissolution of the monasteries by King Henry VIII. Perhaps the most ambitious 'faux' ruin ever created exists today in the garden at Eleutherian Mills, Delaware, where a previous owner, Frank Crowninshield, spent years making a slope below the main residence into a series of ruins, complete with reproductions of Greek and Roman statuary.

When contemplating a new ruin, make it safe (with no loose masonry or stairways without hand-rails) since they are a magnet for children, and should not become an 'attractive nuisance' for someone to injure themselves.

Follies are garden structures that often evoke the appearance of an historical ruin such as a Scottish castle, and are sometimes used to camouflage an unsightly view, but usually have no special purpose except to add an exotic or sinister aura to a garden.

1

2

3

4

5

6

1 *Old monastery arch, Tresco Abbey Gardens, UK.*
2 *Crowninshield Garden, Delaware.* 3 *Sissinghurst Castle towers from white garden, UK.* 4 *Tower, Tor House garden, California.* 5 *Agastache and ruin, Chanticleer Garden, Pennsylvania.* 6 *Crowninshield Garden, Delaware.*

Sculptures and weathervanes

SCULPTURES AND WEATHERVANES Sculpture in the garden can take many forms, including statues (see page 168), which are reproductions of people, and weathervanes which are mostly wood or metal devices for telling in which direction the wind is blowing. Sculpture, as distinct from statuary, can take the form of animals and birds, and it can be abstract, even using elements taken directly from nature, such as smooth river stones placed on pedestals, and driftwood polished by salt and sea spray.

Andy Goldsworthy and Ian Hamilton Finlay are two prominent British sculptors at the forefront of garden art. Goldsworthy scours wilderness forests for sinuous vines, and riverbeds for smooth boulders to create organic art suitable for garden display. Finlay likes to engrave poignant messages on slabs of stone and weatherbeaten barn sidings for display in his Scottish garden, Little Sparta.

Abstract sculpture can make beautiful accents, not only for intimate spaces such as a patio, but at the end of a corridor or vista, and even in wall niches.

The placement for garden sculpture has been debated at length by art curators and horticulturists, resulting in divergent opinions. Though gardening is considered an art form when plants are used to paint the landscape, curators

1 Modernistic sculpture in a courtyard garden. 2 Burle Marx garden, Carmago estate, Brazil. 3 Weathervane and clematis vine. 4 Mud sculpture, Heligan garden, UK.

4

3

don't usually like flowering plants to detract from sculpture, and so sculpture gardens tend to use mostly foliage as green backdrops against which to admire the art. Much of Goldsworthy's and Finlay's art seems best displayed in a misty or monochromatic setting.

Sculpture should not only reflect a garden theme (for example, stone lanterns for a Japanese garden, Rodin-like lovers for a French formal garden, and bronze boars for an Italian); it should also be in scale with its surroundings. Sculpture can be displayed on pedestals, in wall niches, or as fountains. At the Grounds for Sculpture Garden, Hamilton, New Jersey, hundreds of pieces of sculpture are on show in a park-like setting, some on permanent display, others as temporary exhibits. Each of the exhibits is sited in a garden setting specially designed to complement the sculpture.

Weathervanes are sculptural elements that mostly embellish outbuildings such as gazebos and barns. In addition to pointing the direction from which the wind is blowing, their design will often reflect an ethnic theme for a garden, or its location – for example, a rooster might identify a farm garden, a horse maybe a breeding ranch, a dolphin a coastal location. A weathervane can also reflect the interests of the owner – maybe a horse and jockey for a racing enthusiast.

1 Henry Moore-style sculpture, Grounds for Sculpture, New Jersey. 2 Ceramic bamboo, Chanticleer garden, Pennsylvania. 3 Dinosaur egg sculpture. 4 Mud sculpture, Heligan garden, UK.

Shade gardens

SHADE GARDENS Given the choice, most people would rather live in a sunny location than a shady one, and inhabitants of the plant kingdom seem to feel the same way since there is a much wider choice of ornamental plants for sunny locations than for shade. Moreover, the deeper the shade the more problematical it is to find suitable plants, especially flowering kinds.

A big difficulty with gardening in shade is not only the degree of shade, but also poor soil – especially under trees whose roots lie close to the surface and steal all the nourishment. Often, the simple procedure of creating a raised bed with a circle of tree branches or stones will allow good topsoil to be carted in and a suitable planting surface established. However, try to keep the topsoil away from tree trunks by creating a depression around them, since covering too much of a trunk with soil can induce rot.

There are many kinds of shade – light shade, filtered or dappled shade, deep shade, morning, noon and afternoon shade, low shade, high shade, moist shade and dry shade. Moreover, plants identified on nursery labels as 'shade

1 Contrast of light and shade, Whaley Garden, Charleston, South Carolina. 2 Bold contrasts of hosta, astilbe and eunonymus. 3 Shaded formal pool, Winterthur, Delaware.

1

3

2

1

2

tolerant' may grow successfully in light or dappled shade, but fail in deep shade or moist shade where only ferns and moss are likely to thrive. Plants can be so sensitive to the amount of available light that even in a heavily shaded area, where little seems to grow, the removal of a single overhead tree branch can make the difference between no flowers and abundant bloom. Laying down a mulch of white pebbles or painting nearby walls white may also help.

Planting for shade is challenging, but visitors to gardens invariably gravitate to shady locations on warm days, and will linger there longer if there are interesting plantings, even when floral color is sparse. Good foliage contrasts can make up for lack of floral color, particularly when different colors of foliage are supplemented by varied textures and leaf shapes. An appealing leaf contrast might be silvery Japanese painted fern and blue-leafed 'Blue Angel' hostas. An example of textural contrasts might be velvety lady's-mantle leaves and the lustrous, leathery foliage of hellebores. Good leaf contrasts result by pairing feathery maidenhair fern and the slender arching blades of Japanese wood grass.

3

6

Some plant families have leaves as colorful as any flower: coleus includes bright red, pink, chartreuse, orange and yellow in its color range, while caladiums offer all shades of red, plus white and bi-colors that include several shades of green. Though both these are tender, coleus can be raised inexpensively from seed each year, and caladium bulbs store easily indoors in a frost-proof area during winter. Among coleus varieties, the 'Saber' series is naturally basal-branching and requires little or no pinching to delay going to seed because it is naturally late flowering. Shade from tall trees or tall buildings can produce the best conditions for growing shade-tolerant plants like azaleas and rhododendron (see page 149) because high shade provides the air circulation they enjoy. For more advice on planting in woodland, see page 217.

The showiest summer annuals for shade include impatiens, tuberous begonias, wax begonias and wishbone flower (*Torenia*). 'Non-stop' tuberous begonias can be raised inexpensively from seed and since they predominate in red, pink, yellow and orange tones they can present a colorful impact when massed along a path. Good hardy flowering perennials for shade include forget-me-not, dame's rocket, hellebore, trillium and primulas. Hardy bulbs to consider include bluebells, winter aconites and cyclamen.

1 *Contrast of deciduous trees and evergreens, autumn.*
2 *Leaf contrasts from mostly maidenhair fern, violas and hostas.* **3** *Woodland shade garden at Cedaridge Farm.*
4 *Shady nook, Stellenberg garden, South Africa.* **5** *Side garden with hostas and caladiums.* **6** *Bronze heart-shaped leaves of ligularia 'Othello' dominate a Christchurch, New Zealand, shade garden.*

An impressive shade garden in the USA is Winterthur, Delaware, home of the late Henry duPont. A section of garden called The Enchanted Woods features a 'March Walk'. This is a broad curving path that follows a stream between wooded hillsides where sweeps of shade-loving flowering plants begin blooming in March beneath towering tulip poplar trees (*Liriodendron tulipifera*). It is an amazing sight to see so early in the season floral gems such as snow irises, snow crocus, snowdrops, blue squill, yellow aconites, windflowers, all blooming amid drifts of perennial Lenten rose, and in company with early-flowering shrubs like Judas trees, magnolia, witch hazel and winter hazel. In Europe the coastal garden of Le Vasterival, the Normandy home of Princess Greta Sturdza, is superb for its pleasing plant partnerships under shady conditions. All the shade in this valley garden is produced by a high tree canopy, and the Princess attributes much of her success to digging a $50 hole for a $10 plant.

Generally speaking, less than six hours of direct sunlight is considered a shady location, but soil temperature will affect plant performance. Many plants – like garden lilies, primulas and clematis – will tolerate shade only if their roots can be kept cool. Adding moisture-retentive humus to the soil (in the form of leaf mold or garden compost preferably) will help these shade-lovers through hot summers.

The half-acre shade garden of Paul Cezanne at Aix-en-Provence features mostly foliage effects, branch configurations, and attention to shadow patterns. It includes a shaded courtyard and paths leading off into thickets of mock orange, the lower branches pruned to create leafy tunnels that lead to islands of light from clearings in the roof canopy.

1 *Shade-tolerant Japanese woodland grasses and forget-me-nots, Cedaridge Farm.* **2** *Tender clivia massed beneath dawn redwoods.* **3** *Barnhaven primulas color a small shade garden at Cedaridge Farm.*

3

2

Shadow patterns

SHADOW PATTERNS can produce decorative lines similar to silhouettes, but across lawns and walls, breaking up the monotony of large expanses of grass or stonework. When the sun is low on the horizon, such as sunrise and sunset, it can shine through trees and structures to streak the landscape with long shadows.

The drama of lawn shadows is particularly noticeable at Middleton Place Gardens, South Carolina, where a series of lawn terraces descends a gentle slope, creating strong horizontal shadows between a pair of lakes shaped like butterfly wings.

The late Roberto Burle Marx, Brazilian landscape architect, orchestrated shadow patterns against a wall he designed beside his veranda at his home and garden near Rio de Janeiro. The flat wall of large granite blocks was inspired by walls he saw among Inca ruins, the face of the wall placed deliberately so that the feathery fronds of adjacent palm trees cast their ephemeral shadow patterns over it as the sun moves across the sky.

1

2

3

1 *Morning shadow patterns, Cedaridge Farm.* 2 *Butterfly lakes, Middleton Place Gardens, South Carolina.* 3 *Maple leaf lawn shadows.* 4 *Palm shadow on Burle-Marx wall, Brazil.*

4

Shell designs

SHELL DESIGNS in gardens are generally used to decorate walls of grottoes because exposure to sun quickly discolors them. Shells harvested fresh from the sea can be extraordinarily beautiful – white and pink in the conch, orange, red and pink in scallops, even black and blue with mussels. Also, the diversity of shapes is extraordinary, from rounded abalone and paua shells, to long, narrow razor shells, allowing them to be used like mosaic tiles to create intricate designs, even the shapes of flowers, birds and human forms.

A recently completed design in shells can be seen at Tresco Abbey Gardens, the Isles of Scilly, where the interior of a gazebo is decorated with shells that make floral arrangements. Since Tresco is a coastal garden and the theme for the terraced garden with the gazebo is Mediterranean, the shell designs are most appropriate. However, what makes the feature more appealing than the actual artistry of the designs is the fact that the colors are echoed in the adjacent plantings – maroon-colored mussels match the succulent dark red leaves of *Aeonium arboreum* 'Swartkop', and a dusky-pink sedum repeats the pink of scallop shells.

1 *Shell grotto, Nassau Botanical Garden, Bahamas.*
2 and 5 *Shell mosaics, Tresco Abbey Gardens, UK.* 3 *Shell mosaics, Old Westbury garden, New York State.* 4 *Shell mosaic, Kerdalo garden, France.*

1

2

3

5

4

Silhouettes

SILHOUETTES are usually natural lines or forms produced by back-lighting. They help to decorate a skyline, especially at dusk and dawn, and stand out against light-colored backgrounds such as a whitewashed wall or a fall of snow. Dramatic silhouettes are produced by tree trunks as straight as a pencil, and snaking, coiling forms like the tortuous branches of a Japanese maple, especially when the background is muted by mist.

Although silhouettes can be produced artificially, for example by metal grillwork and woven bamboo, opportunities to take advantage of natural silhouettes are boundless. It may require little more than the clearing of undergrowth to isolate a gnarled, twisted tree trunk, or a coiling wisteria vine, and just a little judicious pruning will dramatize the silhouette.

Silhouettes are not only decorative accents to admire for their interesting lines, but also useful as framing elements, the slender straight trunks of a pine and radiating side branches, for example, helping to enclose a distant view in a natural border.

1 *Branch silhouette, golden form of Norway maple, Le Vasterival, France.* 2 *Monterey cypress, Rathmoy, New Zealand.* 3 *Morning skyline silhouettes, Middleton Place, South Carolina.* 4 *Live oaks, Live Oak Plantation, Louisiana.* 5 *Japanese maple branch silhouette, Winterthur, Delaware.*

1

2

3

5

4

Sitting areas and hammocks

SITTING AREAS AND HAMMOCKS In addition to benches on which one can pause and rest during a garden walk, gardens need areas with seats for meetings and entertaining. The beauty of a sitting area is that it can become a popular destination within the garden. Seats, with or without a table, can be grouped for relaxation and reading, to watch the world go by in a busy city, or to admire panoramas, sunrises and sunsets. Sitting areas can be open to the sky, strategically sited on a lawn area or paving. Alternatively, they can be placed inside shelters like gazebos.

When a sitting area is needed for outdoor dining it can be rustic – a pair of wooden seats with a picnic table, for example, set a good distance from the house – or it can be located conveniently near to the dining room or kitchen. At Tresco Abbey Gardens, in the Isles of Scilly, there is a stone table with a slab seat that many visitors use for eating picnic lunches. Few realize that the table itself is a sacrificial altar once used by Druids in their pagan ceremonies.

A seat for admiring a view may not be the best type of seat for dining at a table. For example, in the USA a popular item of outdoor furniture for viewing scenery is called an Adirondack seat, featuring a steep wooden seat that inclines back to relax the body. It positions the body too low and too far back for comfortable dining at a table, but wide arm rests make the Adirondack seat suitable for resting drinks and plates for snacking and picnics. The same is true of rocking chairs. Though comfortable for relaxing, they are awkward for pulling up to a table, and are best used to admire a view, such as from a veranda.

Hammocks are the ultimate in relaxation, especially when one wishes to doze or quietly listen to birdsong. Hammocks can be strung between two trees or between sturdy posts. At the Bitter End Yacht Club, Virgin Gorda, a rope hammock is even positioned inside a 'castaways' shelter made from beach stones and a thatched roof. The hammock provides a beautiful elevated view of the Caribbean, while the shelter provides shade for reading.

1

2   3

4

5

1 *Outdoor dining circle, Rathmoy, New Zealand.* 2 *Adirondack seats, Blueberry Hill, Vermont.* 3 *Hammock alcove, Bitter End Yacht Club, Virgin Gorda.* 4 *Sheltered dining alcove, Capetown.* 5 *Picnic table and seat, Tresco Abbey Gardens, UK.*

Staking

STAKING is necessary in order to keep many kinds of plants erect, not merely vines like morning glories and climbing roses, which need some form of support in order to climb, but also tall, tapering plants like delphinium and hollyhock and top-heavy plants like tuberous dahlias. Even bushy plants like peonies, when the large flowers are wet with rain, will need staking.

Some forms of staking are preferred over others. For example, a cat's cradle of wire or string to support peony flowers soon becomes hidden by foliage. Other forms of staking may be visible, but decorative, for example bamboo stakes to stake individual spires of delphinium; trelliswork for training climbing roses; rustic teepees made from willow, and slatted cages in the form of pyramids to grow clematis.

For vegetable gardens, staking can be more utilitarian, for example using strong wire cylinders to make tomato vines self-supporting, and netting to grow pole beans.

In deciding a method of staking climbers, consider the habit of the plant to be supported. Sweet peas, for example, are self-supporting when planted against trellis or netting, using tendrils to climb. Tendrils, however, will not grip a flat surface like a wall. Trumpet creepers, on the other hand, have aerial roots that can grip a flat porous surface like brick, but will collapse when the surface is smooth or polished. 'Climbing' roses is really a misnomer since most varieties need their canes tied to sturdy supports in order to climb. In the wild the hooks on their thorns do allow them to push their canes through tree branches, but otherwise tying with string or twist-ties is needed to keep their canes growing aloft over arches and arbors.

Claude Monet liked to grow shrub roses as standards, or tree-form. Regular tree-form roses, such as hybrid teas grafted to a straight stem, and self-supporting, were not satisfactory, as the blooms were generally too sparse, so he had special metal supports custom-made by a metalworker to create a wire umbrella so shrub roses, with their enormous number of flowers, could be used as the top-knot, spreading out and creating an avalanche of flowers without the stems breaking.

An often-overlooked method of staking is the natural support that a tree can give to a vine, particularly clematis which will twine high into the topmost branches. English ivy has aerial roots that will grip tree bark, and cloak a trunk from the ground up. It is not parasitic, and providing the tree is healthy, the ivy will seldom harm it.

1 *Rustic teepee for hop vine.* 2 *Japanese-style brace to support heavy willow branch.* 3 *Wire cat's cradle to support peonies.* 4 *Metal umbrella frame to support rose canes, Monet's garden.* 5 *Bamboo stakes for pole beans.* 6 *Slender birch branches to support delphinium.*

Statuary

STATUARY is usually considered to be lifelike reproductions of people, as distinct from sculpture in general which covers lifelike reproductions of many kinds, including animals, and also abstract forms. Many garden owners dislike statuary in a garden, but will allow abstract sculptural art, believing that realistic statues make a garden look like a cemetery. Monet disliked sculpture of any kind in the garden, particularly statues. His friend, Renoir, though, intended his most famous statue, Venus Victorious, as a garden ornament, even designing a columned water garden in which to place her (though he died before the plan could be implemented). Statuary works well in gardens intended to evoke a classical theme, such as Italian baroque, Ancient Greek or Roman. It also suits gardens with an ecclesiastical aura, such as a medieval herb plot where statues of the patron saint of gardening, Saint Fiacre, are popular.

Pairs of statues – such as a couple of sphinxes or two maidens – can look appealing at the entrance to a garden, depending on how ostentatious its owner wants to be. One of the most charming sculpture gardens in the classical tradition is Jasmine Hill, Alabama, where the garden evokes the sensation of visiting a Greek ruin. Marble reproductions of classical Greek statues command prominent positions within an area of theme gardens, the Head of Hera facing a water-lily pool and Winged Victory resting on a pedestal in a rose garden.

When placing statuary, realize that a statue needs to be large enough to be noticed, but not so large as to overwhelm the space. Pay attention to appropriateness – for example, an Oriental statue for a Japanese or Chinese garden and Roman statue for an Italian garden. There are times when statuary is chosen to deliberately shock people or produce an eerie feeling. An image of Medusa with her hair coiling with snakes adds a deliberately macabre element to a ruin at Eleutherian Mills, Delaware. An Italian marble carving of Leda and the Swan shows the Greek goddess coupling with her lover in the form of a swan at Hever Castle, England. The Three Muses, showing three naked Greek women embracing each other, is a popular feature of a terrace at Hearst Castle, California.

1 Aborigine sentinels, Rickett's Sanctuary, Australia. 2 Roman busts flank a Greek god, Plas Brondanw, Wales. 3 Replica of Manet's famous painting, Le Déjeuner sur l'Herbe, Grounds for Sculpture, New Jersey. 4 Easter Island statue, Ngamamaku garden, New Zealand. 5 Sphinx sentinels, Cranbrook, Michigan. 6 Snow-covered Buddha. 7 Memorial statue, Villa Taylor, Morocco. 8 Roman bust, Glen Burnie, Virginia.

2

4

3

Stepping stones

STEPPING STONES are useful to cross shallow water and boggy ground, though they should never tax a person's ability to balance from one stepping stone to another by presenting too wide a gap between stones or too long a section. Even along a footpath with the stones firmly seated in soil and barely protruding above ground level, a long strand of stepping stones can look unnatural and cause dizziness, except in a mountainous landscape, such as an alpine garden, where they may blend in well with outcroppings of rock.

The shape for stepping stones is usually round, though square and rectangular ones work well in formal gardens. A rough texture will prevent a slippery surface when wet. For stability, stepping stones need to be firmly seated. When crossing water, it is even advisable to first drain the site and seat the stones in a concrete foundation.

One of the most beautiful gardens enhanced by stepping stones is the Oehme Alpine Gardens, Washington State, USA, where long stretches of natural stone are used to form steps and stepping stones that alternate to negotiate a spectacular garden built along the sides of a mountain.

Millstones, and replicas of millstones, make good stepping stones. These feature prominently in traditional Japanese gardens.

1

2

3

5

1 *Ingenious use of Belgian block.* 2 *Thyme-bordered stepping stones.* 3 *Stepping stone path across lawn, Butchard Gardens, Canada.* 4 *Millstones, Japanese garden.* 5 *Stepping stones, Japanese Garden, Seattle Arboretum.*

Steps and stiles

STEPS AND STILES Steps are a means of negotiating a steep slope in comfort and a connection between two levels (see page 123). They can add strength to a landscape and point the direction in which to head next. Steps can be bold and ornamental, look strong and natural – as in Japanese gardens – or show decoration such as Spanish tile work. However, a flight of steps should not be too long before producing a place to pause and rest, like a terrace or landing. Avoid making steps that continue for more than 6 ft. of height before providing a landing. Also, broad steps are generally safer than narrow steps.

Though stone and brick are the primary materials used for steps because of durability, steps can be made from wood and a combination of materials, such as wooden landscape ties and gravel. Steps made from all wood or all metal (such as a spiral or straight design), are generally called stairs, and they should feature a handrail for safety and comfort. A non-slip surface and night lighting are also important considerations for both steps and stairs.

Grass is among the least durable paving surface for steps, since it will wear out from heavy use. This is especially true if the steps are narrow, but a broad flight of grass steps that is not subjected to heavy wear can look extremely restful.

1 *Stone steps, Bishop's Close garden, Portland, Oregon.*
2 *Porch steps, Monet's garden.* 3 *Stepped rock garden, Glencoe Farm, Pennsylvania.* 4 *Italianate steps, Blake House, California.*

1

2

3

4

Ramps provide an alternative to steps where the grade is not too steep, to provide mower or wheelchair access. However, ramps take up more space than steps, and unless the ramp is made to zig-zag it is impractical for steep slopes.

The vertical part of a step is called a 'riser', while the horizontal part is called a 'tread.' As a general rule, the maximum riser height should not exceed 6 ½ in. and the minimum tread depth should be 11 in. Uniformity is extremely important for formal steps. Though the tread width and depth can vary for an informal flight, like access to a beach and into a ravine, the riser height should be as consistent as possible.

A garden with a distinctive step design is Neptune's Walk in the Tresco Abbey Gardens, Isles of Scilly. The flight, starting at the bottom of a quarry garden, ascends straight as an arrow, connecting several terraces before reaching the top where a figurehead of King Neptune stares out across the gardens on a stone pedestal. A similar flight of steps in the USA extends down a hillside and up the other side to a swan fountain at Tyreconnell, Baltimore, creating a spectacular vista from the main house across a valley. It was inspired by steps forming the central axis at the Villa d'Este, near Rome. Dumbarton Oaks, Washington DC, includes an imposing flight of horseshoe steps leading from the main house to a swimming pool.

1 *Swiss Pines Japanese Garden, Pennsylvania.* **2** *Grass steps, woodland garden.* **3** *Steps using circular pavers.* **4** *Ornate metal balustrade.* **5** *Liriope-edged brick steps.* **6** *Horseshoe steps, Dumbarton Oaks, Washington DC.* **7** *Spiral stairway, Le Petit Hameau, Versailles.* **8** *Ivy-edged steps.*

1

2

3

4

5

6

7

8

1

2

3

One of Monet's early gardens was at Vétheuil, a few miles south of his present restored garden at Giverny. At Vétheuil he cultivated a steep slope leading from his front door to the banks of the River Seine. A terraced section provided space for a cutting garden, where a steep descent of steps was used to grow nasturtiums across the pavers from the edges. The effect of vertical yellow sunflowers and horizontal orange nasturtiums in the cutting garden can be seen in his painting entitled *The Artist's Garden at Vétheuil*.

Stiles are the simplest of steps to negotiate a fence or wall. They are frequently encountered on walks through the countryside where livestock is penned, for a stile will allow a person to climb over without having to open a gate. At Cedaridge Farm there is a stile copied from a farm on the Yorkshire Moors, giving access to a fenced-in orchard. It features two boards set at angles to each other, allowing people to straddle the top rail of the fence, using a protruding wooden handle for balance. At Glen Burnie garden, Virginia, there is a handsome stone stile for climbing a stone wall, similar to stiles common in Wales, where selected stones are cantilevered and protrude strategically to form steps.

1 *Formal stairway leading to woodland.* 2 *Stone wall with cantilevered steps.* 3 *Wooden stile at Cedaridge Farm.*
4 *Timber risers and gravel treads edge a stream.*

4

Streams and spillways

STREAMS AND SPILLWAYS. Streams are watercourses that can meander through a garden to introduce the sound of running water and also glittering water reflections. On flat ground they may pass placidly through a garden in pronounced wide curves, while on slopes they can gush, trickle, and tumble as they descend. To create a natural-looking stream, first investigate wild streams. Notice the type of stones and their natural placement, and photograph any interesting cascades, shallows and waterfalls as a reference.

Streams that run through woodland may be able to support luxurious moss and fern growth. At Cedaridge Farm the sunny side of a stream is maintained as lawn sloping to the water's edge, and the other side is shadowy woodland, the two areas connected by a bridge. As well as bridges, good structural accents for streams include stepping stones, boulders, and millwheels. The edges can feature observation decks and gazebos.

1

2

3

5

1 *Japanese style rill.* 2 *Curving canal, Callaway Gardens, Georgia.* 3 *Mossy rocks along meandering stream, Swiss Pines Japanese garden, Pennsylvania.* 4 *Series of spillways, Monteiro garden, Brazil.* 5 *Natural stream and mill, Cutalossa Farm, Pennsylvania.*

4

1

2

3

4

5

Where a stream does not already exist on a property it can be made artificially by excavating a watercourse and lining it with a flexible liner, the latter itself hidden by pebbles or sand. Nor does a stream need a natural source, such as a spring, since the water can be trucked to the site and re-circulated by means of a pump through a filter to keep it clean.

Spillways are overflow channels from dams along streams that back up the water to form a pond or to create a boggy area for the growing of a rich assortment of moisture-loving plants, like Japanese and flag iris, candelabra primroses and Chilean gunnera. Spillways also slow the water flow to create limpid pools for the growing of waterlilies.

1 *Stream edged with gunnera and ferns, Christchurch park, New Zealand.* 2 *Stream and bridge, Cedaridge Farm.* 3 *Stream with waterlilies, Clos Coudray, France.* 4 *Meandering stream, Innisfree garden, New York State.* 5 *Irises, azaleas and hostas edge a stream at Trott's Garden, New Zealand.* 6 *Path-bordered stream, Glenfalloch, New Zealand.*

6

Summerhouses and pavilions

SUMMERHOUSES AND PAVILIONS 'Summerhouse' is a term that embraces a number of garden buildings designed to view the garden in comfort. It can be located close to the main residence or at some distance, as a quiet retreat. Aesthetically, summerhouses are a step up from a gazebo, usually glassed-in, with furniture, even a library, and although many have no heat, they can be heated for year-round enjoyment and growing potted plants.

Many different styles of summerhouse exist. They can look like a Victorian-style gingerbread gazebo, an Oriental tea-house, a Greek temple or a Roman villa. Summerhouses also sometimes do double duty as bath-houses, with an open façade onto the swimming pool and rear cabana space for changing.

Another popular name for a summerhouse is 'pavilion', which in Islamic gardens was often a colonnaded building overlooking a garden and used for entertaining. Pavilions frequently feature drapes across the front so they have an Islamic look, and sometimes are designed entirely of canvas to resemble a nomadic tent.

1

1 Chinese pavilion, Glen Burnie, Virginia. 2 Orangerie-style pavilion, Glen Burnie, Virginia. 3 Canvas pavilion, Christchurch, New Zealand. 4 English summerhouse, Long Melford, UK.

2

3

4

Sundials

SUNDIALS are instruments for telling time from shadows cast by the sun as it traverses the sky. They have been in use since at least 1500 BC. A sundial's distinguishing feature is a dial face marked with hours, and a protrusion known as a style to cast a shadow across the dial.

Horizontal dials are the most common, made from stone or bronze and mounted on a pedestal. These can be any geometric shape, but mostly round or square, and are frequently used in herb gardens as a focal point. Vertical sundials are designed for mounting on a wall, and are most often seen on ruins and stone towers, especially in historical gardens of French chateaux, Scottish castles and monasteries.

Many sundials have the additional attraction of an inscription. A particularly whimsical inscription can be seen on a sundial at the Ladew Topiary Gardens, Maryland, which reads: 'I am a sundial and I make a botch of what is done, far better with a watch.'

1 and 5 Herb gardens with sundial embellishment.
2 and 3 Perennial gardens with sundials. 4 Historic herb garden with sundial at Butler Point, New Zealand.

1

2

3

4

5

Swimming pools and hot tubs

SWIMMING POOLS AND HOT TUBS Swimming pools in summer seem to draw people like a warm hearth and log fire does in winter. The surrounding area of the pool itself can be such a good place for entertaining groups of people outdoors, it's tempting not only to have the adjacent ground pleasantly landscaped, but also to feature a bar for serving drinks. A Polynesian-style tiki bar, with bamboo beams and roof thatched with rattan, would be one possible design for this purpose.

Swimming pools can be a jarring interruption on the landscape unless the pool is properly situated and its harsh outline softened with plants. This is particularly true of traditional rectangular pools featuring sky-blue water that can look as unattractive as a blue plastic sheet laid flat on a lawn. Conventional swimming pools can be so foreign in the landscape, it's a wonder that more people do not favor a natural-looking pool design. Kurt Bluemel, a US nurseryman specializing in ornamental grasses, at his home near Baltimore installed a freeform shape overhung with stone slabs and boulders to create what appears to be a natural rock pool, the stone softened by the wispy, arching leaf blades of bold ornamental grasses such as maiden grass (*Miscanthus sinensis*).

1

2

3

4

1 and 2 *Hot tub and swimming pool with flagstone surround.* **3** *Swimming pool landscaped with trees and shrubs.* **4** *Grasses and boulders create a naturalistic setting.*

There are several ways to make a swimming pool fit comfortably into the landscape:

1 Use an informal design. If you use a formal design, try to echo the architectural lines of the residence.

2 Rather than paint the pool liner white so it reflects blue sky, consider painting it a slate blue or eggplant purple to achieve a more natural reflective surface.

3 Use lots of ornamental grasses in the surrounding landscape, especially to hide any safety fence. The arching leaf blades will help soften the hard lines of the pool. Also, grasses do not attract bees like annuals and perennials, making the landscape safer for people who are allergic to bee stings.

4 Design the pool to look like a wildlife pond or a local natural swimming hole, perhaps using a local flagstone for the pool surround and local boulders to break up the monotony of flat surfaces. Water for the pool can be introduced by a naturalistic waterfall or cascade.

A particularly innovative pool planting is at the Polynesian Spa, Rotorua, New Zealand, where a series of hot springs emerges beside a lake. The hot springs form pools, each with a different temperature. The most popular pool is landscaped all around with native plants, though under normal circumstances even native plants could not survive there because of sulfurous gases that can poison roots. To prevent this, a rubber membrane is buried beneath the topsoil to divert such gases away.

Jacuzzis or hot tubs can be part of a swimming-pool complex, or they can be a stand-alone installation to provide the hot-spring experience. Though there are many commercial brands, most are simply square or circular raised baths with a tile or plastic liner, and these are of little or no decorative value in a garden setting. For that reason they are often confined to decks. However, hot tubs can be designed to look

2

1

1 *Formal swimming pool, Virginia Robinson garden, California.* **2** *Circular pool with parterres.* **3** *Swimming pool beside the Delaware River, Pennsylvania.* **4** *Terraced swimming pool.* **5** *Hot springs pool, Polynesian Spa, New Zealand.* **6** *Infinity pool, Buccaneer Resort, St. Croix.* **7** *Potted exotics create a tropical theme.*

7

3

6

5

4

1 *French-style bathhouse, Chanticleer garden, Pennsylvania.* 2 *Tropical pool, Auckland.* 3 *Raised lap pool.*

natural, especially when disguised with stone to resemble a rock pool.

New Zealanders are enterprising gardeners and they have discovered an inexpensive way to emulate a hot spring. Called a 'bush bath', this consists of a heavy enamel bathtub set over a fire pit. After the tub is filled from a garden hose, a pile of logs is lit under the bath to heat the water. Though the water could be brought to boiling, one learns quickly how big to make the fire to create a comfortable water temperature. A New Zealand bush bath at Cedaridge Farm is located at the rear of a guest cottage among junipers and ostrich ferns.

'Infinity' pools are popular wherever the site overlooks a large body of water such as the sea, a lake or a river. Unobtrusive low, thin walls can be used for the pool and this lessens the visual separation between it and the natural water feature beyond. Water spilling over the edge into a hidden channel on the far side helps hide the wall itself, further making it appear as if the pool is an extension of the watery background.

At Cedaridge Farm there is a wildlife pond that also does double duty as a swimming pond. A nearby barn serves as a changing room, and steps allow easy access to the pond. After introduction via a waterfall, the water is kept clean by being re-circulated through a filter. Boulders and colonies of flag iris surround the margin, and even a waterlily or two, confined to submerged planters, decorate the pond surface. Wild deer, turkeys and birds emerge from adjacent woodland to drink at the pond, but its primary purpose is to provide a tranquil place for humans to swim during summer.

Tapestry gardens

TAPESTRY GARDENS feature plantings for predominantly foliage effect. They came into vogue after the early French Impressionist painters painted landscapes vibrant with different foliage colors. Visitors to the restored gardens of Claude Monet at Giverny and Cezanne at Aix-en-Provence can see today how these enthusiastic gardeners and keen observers of nature looked beyond fleeting floral color to decorate the skyline by using not only foliage color contrasts, but also taking into account leaf texture, trunk and branch configurations, as well as a plant's characteristic form. Thus they highlighted weeping effects from trees like willows by siting these next to columnar trees such as fastigiate oaks and poplars.

Cezanne especially preferred to rely on trees and shrubs not noted for showy flowers. He disliked to see man's domination of nature and reveled at the sight of nature reclaiming man's intrusion – for example, crumbling walls cloaked in ivy, trees with roots forcing through flagstone, ruins shrouded in curtains of leaves. Above all, he liked to discover in the landscape contrasts of leaf color and form, such as silvery-gray olive leaves on sinuous branches beneath black-green foliage of umbrella pines with a spreading leaf canopy, the red clay soil and reddish bark of the pines adding further interest.

In addition to selecting trees for skyline effect, the artistic gardener will apply similar criteria to the choice of lower-growing plants for beds, borders and container groupings. These include annuals such as multi-colored coleus and silvery dusty miller, perennials such as shiny artemisia and golden feverfew, and shrubs such as red barberry and golden privet. By contrasting needle evergreens such as blue spruce and gold-leaf false cypress with broadleaf evergreens such as dark green holly and the lustrous leaves of rhododendron, the enchanting understated color combinations will endure through winter months.

The shape and habit of growth of a plant is also extremely important when putting together a tapestry effect, especially along the skyline. In Monet's garden, for example, the west side of his pond features the cloud-like shape of a golden weeping willow, a column-like pair of green Lombardy poplars, the billowing form of a copper beech, and the yellow, feathery stems of bamboo. Even when a yellow-flowered laburnum and a blue wisteria bloom beneath the trees in May, it is the majesty of the trees and their juxtaposition that dominates to produce a varicolored skyline and the bonus of a richly colored water reflection.

1 *Valley garden, Maple Glen, New Zealand.* 2 *Skyline trees, Monet's water garden.* 3 *Bold foliage contrasts beside a patio.* 4 *Woodland garden, Bois des Moutiers, France.*

1 *Tapestry hillside, Kerdalo garden, Britanny.* 2 *Tapestry garden, The Garden House, UK.* 3 *Burle-Marx style tapestry effect, Auckland tropical garden.*

By choosing among predominantly woody plants for the tapestry effects, the range of color can be extensive, covering a hillside, yet the maintenance for such a large area can be minimal, requiring only an occasional pruning and feeding to maintain a luxurious leaf display. A particularly good woody plant to use in a hillside tapestry garden is the bushy Japanese white willow, *Salix integra* 'Hakura-Nishiki'. In spring, the new leaves are so white that from a distance, it looks like a white-flowering ornamental cherry in bloom, with the advantage that the white coloration of the leaves lasts into summer. On an even grander scale, few white variegated trees can compare with the pagoda dogwood, *Cornus alternifolia* 'Argentea'. Particularly striking is the way it holds its branches horizontally, creating a distinctive 'tiered' look.

For sunny small spaces such as patios and decks, the choice of available foliage plants is extensive. For example, one could consider Persian shield (*Strobilanthes*) with silver and purple iridescent leaves that have a metallic shine; velvety licorice plant (*Helichrysum petiolare*) with cascading, silvery oval leaves; striped forms of canna, such as 'Pretoria' (yellow and green) and 'Durban' (red, orange and green), and angel-wing begonias with marbled, sharply-indented leaves. A vast number of ornamental grasses also work well in sunny tapestry gardens.

For shade, there are heucheras with bi-colored, heavily veined, ivy-like leaves; caladiums with bi-colored and tri-colored heart-shaped leaves, no two leaves exactly alike; consider also multi-colored coleus and variegated silver-and-green Swedish ivy. Two good hardy perennial grasses for shade are Bowles golden sedge (*Carex elata* 'Aurea') and Japanese woodland grass (*Hakonechloa macra* 'Aureola'). The former has solid yellow leaf blades, while the latter is gold with an inconspicuous slender green stripe. Both have a cascading habit and are clump forming. They are good to grow in close proximity to blue hostas such as 'Blue Angel' and the silvery Japanese painted fern (*Athyrium niponicum* var. *pictum*). All are suitable for growing outdoors to overwinter, and all look good grouped in pots.

At the French garden of Kerdalo, in Britanny, from a terrace running the length of the main house visitors marvel at a distant hillside planted with trees and shrubs in contrasting leaf colors. Another fine French tapestry garden exists at Parc Floral des Moutiers, in Varengeville. The founder matched leaf colors to swatches of fabric for his designer, and then set about landscaping an entire valley with an extraordinary palette of leaf colors, textures and forms, using trees as big as Atlas cedars, shrubs such as rhododendron and hydrangea, and perennial groundcovers like ostrich ferns and dwarf bamboo. At The Garden House in Cornwall visitors can look down from a tower at a smaller-scale tapestry garden which uses yellow and blue evergreen shrubs as its main components.

Temples

TEMPLES are generally colonnaded shelters that simulate classical Greek and Roman structures. They are similar to gazebos, but invariably made of stone, and they are a much more sophisticated accent to have in the garden. Usually they will feature a statue in the middle as an additional embellishment, such as Diana, the Huntress. Though temples are generally associated with formal design, they are suitable for informal gardens, especially those located in woodland and beside a lake. The Temple of Echo, at Rousham Park, near Oxford, England, faces a ridge of the Cherwell Hills, causing a loud shout from the temple to echo back.

Temples evoke a romantic feeling when encountered unexpectedly. Though costly to purchase from garden supply centers and to build, a romantic appearance can be introduced by creating only a temple façade, using a portico of columns supporting the portico roof against a wall, to evoke a ruin. The ruin can be made to look authentic by growing vines up the columns and scattering broken pieces of column across the ground.

2

1 *Temple of Diana and* (3) *Diana statue, Nemours, Delaware.* 2 *Temple-style gazebo, Larnach Castle, Dunedin.* 4 *Lakeside temple, Morris Arboretum, Pennsylvania.* 5 *Temple of Love, Meadowbrook Farm, Pennsylvania.*

5

Terraces

TERRACES The most challenging site to make a garden is flat ground, because a slope can be terraced to present a dramatic view looking down and, equally, a dramatic view looking up. The trick to making a flat site interesting is to ensure there are lots of corners to negotiate, and to have interesting plant partnerships or structural surprises around every corner. To overlook a slope, terraces can be straight or curved, built of stone or brick. They can be highly ornate, like the four long Italianate terraces at Powys Castle, England, tied together with towering walls of green yew and vines, or they can be simply tiers of flat lawn that descend like graceful steps of green grass. Terraces with hard surfaces can best accommodate furniture for relaxing, a barbecue, hot tub, a fountain and even a hammock or swing seat for admiring a view.

Terraces detached from the house should be considered whenever there is some distance between the main residence and a slope, for example in a coastal location where the house is set back for fear of storm damage. When cost is a consideration, wooden decks can be considered instead of stone terraces. In fact, a wooden deck is preferred to a stone terrace whenever established trees need to be incorporated into the design. Building a deck is much less disruptive around trees, whereas terraces can alter the drainage and soil chemistry to such an extent, even mature trees may be put in peril.

The fabled Hanging Gardens of Babylon, near Baghdad, had a total of ten terraces, with water carried to the topmost one by an arrangement of wooden screws turned by oxen. As the screws twirled skywards, buckets scooped water from a reservoir and conveyed it aloft.

Many of the great Italian Renaissance gardens feature terraced gardens, though none more impressive than the Villa d'Este, near Rome. The dominant design is a main central axis descending a steep slope, with terraces radiating out left and right, the axis composed of a long flight of stone steps. The Italianate garden of Tyrconnell, Maryland, imitates the main axis and terraces at the Villa d'Este, but attempts to surpass it by continuing up a facing slope to end in a sumptuous fountain.

In modern residential properties terraces conjure up visions of brick or flagstone spaces sometimes leading from the living room, and often providing an outdoor area for entertaining before and after dinner. They can be expansive, open to the sun, or intimate and shaded. Some terraces can achieve both by having a wide open area for sunbathing and socializing, and a cool nook for reading and intimate conversation.

1 *Terraces at Powys Castle, UK.* 2 *Flagstone terrace, Tony Schillig garden, Scotland.* 3 *Italianate terrace, Longwood Gardens, Pennsylvania.* 4 *Terrace of orange trees and agapanthus, Renoir's Garden, France.* 5 *Dry landscape terrace, Tresco Abbey Gardens.*

Tool and potting sheds, and outhouses

TOOL SHEDS, POTTING SHEDS AND OUTHOUSES Tool sheds and potting sheds can make wonderful sanctuaries. The interior design is as important as the exterior, for garden sheds not only allow tools to be stored and plants to be potted, they can include brass beds with down comforters for taking a nap, pot-bellied stoves that can boil water for a refreshing cup of tea, even shelves for a library of garden books and novels for quiet reading. They can be marvelous places to escape the frenetic pace of modern life; mysterious domains that are dusty and earthy and filled with pleasant fragrances from herbs drying in the rafters, beautiful old implements adorning the walls, and pigeonholes for fading seed packets and well-thumbed mail-order catalogs.

The exterior of a garden shed can be embellished with climbing roses, spires of hollyhocks and lupins, window-box planters, and weathered wooden siding, the door always left ajar so that one spring morning a pair of twittering swallows might fly in to make a nest among the beams and raise a family – an omen of good luck.

1

2

3

1 Utility building, Palm House, Bermuda, covered in creeping fig. 2 Tool shed with trellis decoration. 3 Maori-style storage shelter, Butler Point, New Zealand.

1

2

In spite of modern plumbing, many gardens feature an out-house, or privy, as a decorative feature, especially in historical gardens where outhouses are part of an authentic restoration, and in herb gardens designed for an old-fashioned appearance. The simplest design is a narrow wooden hut the width of the toilet seat, built over a pit. A window with window box, a half-moon cut-out on the door, and a weathervane on the roof are common embellishments. Privies at the Governor's Mansion, Williamsburg, Virginia, feature substantial red brick walls to echo the house walls, white paned windows, and black slate roofs, with pairs of toilet seats inside.

Pumphouses also merit some decorative treatment when sited in a prominent place in the garden. Alternatively they can be disguised by a green cover of climbers or creepers.

1 French-style outhouse. 2 Unobtrusive toolshed, partially hidden by rhododenron and plume poppy. 3 Substantial stone tool shed, Welcome Farm, Pennsylvania.

3

Topiary

TOPIARY is the art of clipping woody plants into ornamental shapes. Though the use of pruning shears or an electric hedge-trimmer to clip trees and shrubs with dense foliage is the most common way to create topiary, it is quicker to form a wire frame and plant a fast growing creeper like 'Needlepoint' English ivy or baby's tears to cover it.

British and French gardens are noted for fanciful topiary figures. In Britain the oldest and largest display of topiary art is at Levens Hall, Cumbria, dating to 1690 when a Frenchman, a Monsieur Beaumont, created it for Sir James Grahame, the owner. In the USA the Ladew Topiary Gardens are world famous for their hedges, inspired by topiary Ladew saw during foxhunting meets in England. Though these garden spaces are beyond the scope of most gardeners, the garden of Green Animals, in Portsmouth, Rhode Island, is less than an acre in area within a seven-and-a-half acre

1 *Poodle-cut juniper, Filoli garden, California.* 2 *Ivy-covered elephant, Longwood Gardens, Pennsylvania.* 3 *Topiary hunt in yew, Ladew Topiary Gardens, Maryland.* 4 *Horse and rider, weeping spruce, Deerfield Garden, Pennsylvania.*

1

2

3

4

1 *Boxwood parterre and holly topiary, Waterperry garden, UK.* 2 *Levens Hall topiary garden, UK.* 3 *Topiary goose, Bellagio Conservatory, Las Vegas.* 4 *Overall view, Green Animals garden, Rhode Island.*

1

4

2

3

colonial revival garden established by the late Thomas Brayton in 1880. His daughter, Alice, has continued the garden, and has bequeathed it to a local preservation group after her death. Featuring an assortment of topiary animals, it includes a life-size giraffe and elephant, clipped out of privet.

The earliest reference to a topiary garden is by Pliny the Younger (AD 62–113), a gentleman of considerable wealth and culture, who owned several villas. One of these, Tuscum, he described as having a magnificent garden 'with an avenue of box trees cut topiary fashion, into the shapes of animals…'

Boxwood is still the preferred shrub for creating topiary, for it has a dense weave of branches, its small oval leaves are evergreen, and it is slow growing so that one or two clippings a year are generally sufficient to keep it looking clean. Other plants to consider for topiary are the junipers, weeping spruce, Canadian hemlock, Korean boxwood, and Japanese yew.

Tree accents

1

TREE ACCENTS What is it about trees that evoke such admiration? Partly, it seems, trees are natural landmarks and memorials. Because their lifespan is normally much longer than that of humans, they carry their associations from generation to generation and they make everything surrounding them look more natural, a feeling of serenity – 'something in this modern world, which cannot be cherished too highly' to quote landscape architect Thomas D. Church. He further explained, 'Never underestimate the value of a handsome tree. Protect it. Build your house and garden compositions around it, for it offers you shade, shadow, pattern against the sky, protection over your house, a ceiling over your terrace.'

The late H. Thomas Hallowell Jr., the owner of Deerfield Garden, near Philadelphia, typified the attitude of many when he said of his garden, 'For me, trees exist for one purpose – to make a pretty picture.' And what a pretty picture they can make – from the blizzard of pink blossoms produced by an ornamental cherry to the snaking branches and fleecy, fire-bright leaf canopy of a Japanese maple.

The ancient Chinese Zen masters recognized the special beauty of expressive trees. They revered old trees still clinging to life against harsh adversity, especially evergreen pines with hollowed trunks and gnarled branches twisted into bizarre shapes by storms, a few tufts of leaves barely sufficient for survival. If they could not transplant these tenacious survivors into their gardens, artisans adept at pruning could take a young, nursery-grown tree, and using stakes and wires, twist branches to recreate the weather-worn trees, placing the shaped trees on mounds and promontories so their dignity and charm could be best appreciated.

British gardens value old oak trees as garden accents, the Southern USA has its live oaks festooned with Spanish moss, China its sacred ginkgo, Japan its tortuous black pines, coastal California its majestic towering redwoods, France stupendous old olive trees, New Zealand some amazing specimens of native pohutukawa – all trees worthy of isolating in the landscape to make a bold, natural garden accent.

2

3

1 *Weeping beech pruned to create a skirt, Pukemarama garden, New Zealand.* 2 *Sinuous Japanese maple branches accented by snow.* 3 *European white birch, Cobamong Garden, New York State.* 4 *Deck constructed to accommodate a mature gumbo-limbo tree, Point Pleasant Resort, US Virgin Islands.* 5 *Backlit Japanese maple in autumn colors.*

5

4

Tree roots, stumps and wicker

TREE ROOTS, STUMPS AND WICKER Though most trees hide their roots underground, quite a few kinds expose theirs, especially beech and cypress, plus a host of tropical trees like banyans (*Ficus* spp.) that snake their fluted and flanged roots for immense distances. Erosion also will expose the roots of trees, which sometimes then become beautiful decorative sculptural forms, particularly when planted with flowers like diminutive cyclamen, squill, bromeliads and ferns.

A 'stumpery' is a pile of uprooted tree stumps, the roots protruding like the arms of an octopus, allowing the stumps to interlock and create a substantial rustic wall or arch. They are good to place in shady locations like woodland, with ferns, hostas, heucheras and other shade-loving plants in pockets of soil. A single well-weathered tree stump can be used as a beautiful accent piece for a rock garden or coastal garden, especially if the stump has good textural features like gnarled roots and hollows.

Exposed stumps can be carved to make sculptures, while extracted roots and twigs can be entwined to form a pyramid, nests and globes.

Wicker work is the weaving of pliable branches (especially willow) or vines to create ornamentation such as fences, benches, and arbors. They can also be braided to make figures such as deer, heron, geese, even dinosaurs.

1

2

3

4

1 *Tree stump used to create a rustic fence.* 2 *Wicker fence and built-in seat.* 3 *Arch of fox grape vines.* 4 *Moreton Bay figs, Parnell Rose Garden, Auckland.*

Trellis and treillage

1

TRELLIS AND TREILLAGE Trellis is the English term for wooden lattice or metal rods used as support to train plants such as vines off the ground. Monet's garden uses a great deal of trellis of different kinds since he wanted color to extend high above his paths. In the Clos Normand flower garden simple metal cross-pieces allow flowering vines to drape flowers down like a lace curtain. A wooden trellis is laid flat against a high wall for the growing of espaliered pears, while a third kind of arched trellis forms a canopy over the Japanese bridge in his water garden.

In other French gardens, such as Villandry, trellises form obelisks and arbors for growing climbing roses and espaliered fruit trees. Villandry also features flat trellis shaped like a fan to splay rose canes outwards against a wall in a starburst of color.

Treillage is a French term meaning trelliswork, and describes fanciful criss-crossed lattice designs, mostly of wood and often not intended to support plants, but merely to look decorative unadorned. An extensive and diverse use of treillage is found at the Roseraie de l'Hay, west of Paris, where it forms passageways, arbors, arches, porticos and pergolas solely for the support of climbing roses. Panels of treillage can also be incorporated in more solid buildings such as summer-houses and chapels.

2

4

3

1 *Trelliswork accented by snow.*
2 *Lattice church, Gethsemane Gardens, New Zealand.* 3 *Purple and red clematis entwined.* 4 *Trellised walkway.*

Tropical gardens

TROPICAL GARDENS out of doors do not need to be located only in frost-free locations. They can be made in temperate climates, the plants grown in pots and used for a single season to create an exotic effect and then discarded when autumn frosts kill the tender foliage. Alternatively, the plants can be over-wintered indoors in a conservatory or greenhouse and used from year to year. Some favorite plants to create a tropical effect include tree ferns, Kentia palms, bromeliads and orchids (page 128), angel-wing begonias, caladiums, crotons, canna, banana, gingers (notably *Heleconia* spp.), anthurium, hibiscus, spider plants, cacti, and philodendron vines.

The most innovative tropical gardens in recent years have been inspired by the work of the Brazilian landscape architect, the late Roberto Burle Marx, after he realized that exotic gardens in the conservatories of Europe could be grown outdoors in tropical climates. Shortly after setting up business in Rio de Janeiro, Marx landed a dream assignment – the landscaping of a huge property in Petropolis (a mountain resort north of Rio), known as the Monteiro Estate. Marx worked on the garden continuously until his death in 1994.

The Monteiro garden occupies an entire valley floor, with the main house looking up the valley from a hill to a panorama of majestic sugarloaf mountains. Several lakes were made and lawns established up the sides of the valley to the edges of jungle wilderness. The lawns feature vast sweeps of color from yellow daylilies, blue agapanthus, and red coleus. Islands in the lake are sanctuaries for botanical behemoths such as the giant philodendron vine, *Typhodorum lindeyanum*. Massive Amazon waterlily platters that can support the weight of a child float on the lakes; their flowers pervade the

1

8

6

7

2

3

4

air with a pineapple-like perfume. Parrots and swans breed on the islands.

Marx's own house and garden outside Rio is open to the public. Here are walls that look like an Inca ruin, displaying bromeliads. Other hallmarks of his work are pebble mosaics for walkways, simple but substantial Inca-style arches as transitional elements, and strong foliage contrasts.

One of the finest tropical gardens inspired by Marx is that of the late Noel Scotting, near Auckland, New Zealand, on a frost-free hillside. The entrance driveway dips downhill through a tunnel of lush tropical vegetation to a courtyard screened by palms and a hacienda-style homestead. A large pergola draped with vines frames a view from the living-room across a grassy terrace to the Hauraki Gulf. The terrace curves like a horseshoe past giant Brazilian philodendron vines and a dry slope, boldly planted with succulents, cycads and bromeliads, to an arch that echoes the design of the pergola and its massive wooden beams, all imitating the strong, angular geometry of Marx's Brazilian garden designs.

5

Urns

URNS can make wonderful focal points, and they do not need to be planted. Indeed, many kinds of urns cannot be planted because the top is domed for decoration. However, even urns with open tops may be best left unplanted because the dark black hole acts like the hollow of a tree or a cave opening in a cliff – a mysterious void that draws attention. However, if the opening is left open, take care to plug it during winter so the vessel does not fill with water and crack from freezing.

Urns are usually made of stone, such as marble, and terracotta, or metal. If planted, simplicity is key to a good impression – perhaps a creeping sedum spilling over the rim, or a cockade of New Zealand flax stabbing the sky with spiky leaves.

Italian gardens are notorious for featuring decorative urns, on pedestals, as finials on balustrades, as focal points at the end of a pleached alley, but nowhere are urns more evident than in the gardens of Versailles, where hundreds are used on pedestals at the end of avenues and in niches cut into walls and hedges.

Do not be afraid to err on the side of largesse when choosing an urn as a decorative accent. Many coastal or riverside estates use large, conspicuous urns to mark the position of a safe landing place as a navigational aid during inclement weather. Also consider grouping a collection of unplanted urns in a corner of the garden, or on a terrace, especially urns and pottery representing a particular ethnic culture, such as Cretian and Peruvian.

1

7

8

9

1 *Pergola-framed urn on a pedestal, Stellenberg garden, Capetown.* 2 *Dry landscape, Bellevue garden, New Zealand.* 3 *Hillside garden, The Dingle, UK.* 4 *Slate urn, Attadale, Scotland.* 5 *Urn-like font, Chanticleer garden, Pennsylvania.* 6 **and** 8 *Planted urns.* 7 *Urn centerpiece, courtyard, Cranbrook House, Michigan.* 9 *Urn as an herb garden centerpiece, Cedaridge Farm.*

2

3

5

6

4

Vegetable gardens

VEGETABLE GARDENS are generally the most labor-intensive garden spaces, for success is dependent on many factors, including a sunny site, good drainage, a neutral or only slightly-acid fertile soil, shelter from wind, timely weeding, timely supplemental feeding, rigorous pest control, protection from foraging animals, careful variety selection and usually timely irrigation since natural rainfall can be unreliable.

In poor soils, such as those with too much clay or too much sand, compost or well-decomposed animal manures must be carted to the site. This helps break up clay soils that lock up plant nutrients and gives body to sandy soils that tend to drain away water and nutrients too rapidly.

Traditionally, vegetable gardens grow plants in straight rows since this allows for easy cultivation when weeds need to be hoed and booster applications of fertilizer applied. Mulching rows to deter weed growth and conserve moisture is also easy when rows are straight. The same is true of many irrigation systems, especially drip lines that apply beads of moisture to the root zone. For more decorative effect, the incredible parterre garden of Villandry, south of Paris, grows vegetables in square and rectangular blocks to create colorful patterns within low boxwood edging. For small-size gardens a similar system called 'square-foot gardening' or 'block planting' displays vegetables shoulder-to-shoulder for maximum

1

2

3

8

1 *Straight-row plantings, Longwood Gardens, Pennsylvania.* 2 *Raised beds, Leonard Buck Garden, New Jersey.*
3 *Raised beds, Cedaridge Farm.*
4 *Governor's Palace kitchen garden, Colonial Williamsburg.* 5 *Block planting, Cedaridge Farm.* 6 *'Bright Lights' silverbeet, Cedaridge Farm.*
7 *Overall view of kitchen garden, Château de Villandry, France.* 8 *Red kale and urn decorative accent.*

7

4

yields. Square-foot gardening works best when vegetables are grown in raised beds so the extra soil depth allows vegetables sensitive to crowding, like head lettuce, to thrive.

Another space-saving idea is to train vine crops up stakes. For example, a single plant of a pole bean will outyield bush beans sometimes ten-to-one. Staked indeterminate tomatoes will yield more than the bushy, determinate kind. Attractive staking can be introduced, such as bamboo poles arranged to form a teepee or an A frame support.

Decorative elements for vegetable gardens can include an organic mulch to cover bare soil, such as straw, pine needles or woodchips. Vegetable plots can also feature ornaments, such as trellises and arbors, sundials, urns and bee skeps.

Again, taking inspiration from Villandry, gardeners are mixing vegetables with flowers to create 'edible landscapes'. Curly parsley can make an attractive edging for beds and borders, and the multi-colored stalks of 'Rainbow' chard or silver beet looks sensational as a tall, decorative accent in mixed container plantings.

5

6

Vertical gardens

VERTICAL GARDENS are ideal to consider where space is limited, such as in a small city garden, perhaps within a courtyard. Traditionally, vertical gardens are made by mounting a wall with tiers of window boxes and hanging baskets, strategically positioned so that the plants from one planter will merge with another to create a verdant cover. Cascading plants like maidenhair ferns and piggy-back plants ensure that the planters themselves are hidden.

French botanist and scientist Patrick Blanc has made a specialty of designing *murs vegetaux* – vertical gardens, also known as 'living walls'. A professor at the University of Jussieu, Paris, Blanc traveled with his students to study rainforests, and was inspired to create a vertical garden at his home, after realizing that rainforest plants grow from vertical cliff faces and are not rooted in soil. Such plants draw nutrients from pockets of humus trapped in cracks, and also from the humid air. To achieve a sheer foliage effect, Blanc experimented by growing plants in an absorbent felt liner just half an inch thick, draped like a curtain against a wall. He discouraged roots from penetrating the wall and damaging it by draping an impervious sheet of PVC between the felt and the wall.

A nutrient solution drips down through the felt to provide plant roots with moisture and food in the form of a dilute liquid feed; like a hydroponic system, the water and nutrients are re-circulated to create a constantly moist vertical blanket and lush, luxuriant growth. The composition of the nutrient solution is vital, containing ten trace elements such as calcium, magnesium and sulphur in addition to the major nutrients nitrogen, potassium and potash.

Blanc's system was first exhibited in 1994 at the international garden festival at the Château de Chaumont in the Loire Valley, an annual showcase of innovative garden design. It was such a success that he won numerous commissions, including the decoration of an atrium at the Hotel Pershing, in Paris, using mostly tropical plants.

The success of vertical walls depends to a large extent on foliage contrasts, and if hardy varieties are chosen – as opposed to tropical kinds – maintenance is greatly reduced.

1 *Balcony garden using Swedish ivy as a curtain.* 2 Mur vert (green wall) *using felt planter, Hotel Pershing, Paris.*
3 *Vertical garden using baskets, Cedaridge Farm.* 4 *Wall of annual baskets, France.*

1

2

3

4

Vistas

VISTAS are views. The late Thomas D. Church, landscape architect, in *Gardens are for People*, declared, 'Distant views of mountains and water, intimate views of hills and woods, views over cities at night, all have an endless fascination for people.' He warned, however, that the eye is fickle and easily distracted, and so views should have as few obstacles and diverting distractions as possible.

Views can be long corridors of space that open out to glimpse a quiet glade, a sparkling lake or sandy seashore. Also, they can be expansive to provide a wide panoramic view of a river, coastline or mountain range. Some vistas are obvious, and all that is required is the removal of obstructions like brambles and weed trees to establish a beautiful receding greensward leading the eye to a magnificent natural scenic feature. Good places to begin seeking vistas are from the rooms of the main residence, especially bedrooms, the kitchen and dining room.

At other times a beautiful vista may not be obvious. For example, the late Tom Hallowell Jr., owner of Deerfield Garden, near Philadelphia, did not like to walk out of his front door to be confronted with an asphalt driveway that extended in a direct straight line to the main road, so he had the driveway dug up and seeded in grass. Here he put in lines of tulip poplars (*Liriodendron*) underplanted with pink azaleas and pink dogwoods. Where the driveway had entered the road, he screened the view of passing cars with a bushy hedge and in front of it erected a split-rail fence as a rustic focal point. A new driveway was established, making a less

1 *Framed vista, from boxwood hedges and pine canopy.*
2 *Asphalt driveway, Deerfield Garden, Pennsylvania, converted to green vista.* 3 *Lake-view vista, Tyrconnell garden, Maryland.*
4 *Stream-side vista, Le Vasterival, France.*

1

intrusive, more circuitous route to a new entrance on the main road. Hallowell considered a chainsaw his most useful garden implement.

Vistas can become a main axis for a garden, and a main vista can be intersected to create cross axes, each presenting its own vista. Lots of natural and ornamental features can be used to make vistas more appealing if the ultimate view is blocked or unattractive. For example, a gazebo or temple could help block out a view of ugly buildings, or a vista could be terminated in a fountain. Vistas can extend across lakes, streams, ponds and pools, making water reflections decorative landscape features, and continue beyond the banks to disappear into infinity.

Tall trees pruned to arch their branches can be made to frame a vista. When foreground trunks and branches are seen silhouetted they can etch the view with a sinuous or cross-stitch pattern against bright sky, cloud or mist.

Vistas can be made to appear longer, and the focal point more distant by creating an avenue that becomes progressively narrower, forming an elongated triangle. Vistas can extend well beyond the property line to take in a 'borrowed land-scape', including part of someone else's garden, or a historic building such as a church. Thomas Church advised; 'Skip the first impulse to enclose yourself with screen plantings and high walls. Instead, look out at the neighboring property. Someone else is maintaining it and paying taxes on it.'

Vistas can be realized not only by looking out from the windows or terraces of the main residence, but by walking to the limit of the property and looking back so the residence itself becomes the focal point to terminate the vista. The beginning and end of vistas are also perfect sites for benches, temples and gazebos.

1 *Main vista at Brenthurst garden, Johannesburg.* 2 *Main vista, Tyrconnell garden, Maryland.* 3 *Main vista, Cedaridge Farm.* 4 *River vista, Horrell garden, New Zealand.*

2

3

4

Walls and ha-has

WALLS AND HA-HAS Walls traditionally are intended to keep intruders out of gardens, including foraging animals and humans, but over the years they have become so important to good garden design, they are now among the elements that make strong bones for a garden by dividing spaces and creating compartments. This produces a sense of intimacy and shelter. Cezanne was so enthralled by a high stone wall that surrounds his half-acre property in Provence, he produced an abstract painting of it, entitled *The Garden at Les Lauves*, using broad spade-like brushstrokes to simulate stone. This impressive work heralded the art form now known as Cubism. A similar wall has been constructed at Cedaridge Farm as part of a ruin.

Walls can be made of stone or brick, but it is often desirable to temper their hard lines with vines, particularly Virginia creeper, which has beautiful autumn colors, or perhaps evergreen English ivy and flowering *Clematis montana*.

Walls don't have to be tall to form a privacy barrier. For example, in Monet's garden the walls running along the bottom of the garden are only chest-high, set with railings to a greater height to keep out intruders. This then allows passers-by to admire his garden. Most importantly, Monet could also look out over the wall into the bucolic countryside beyond his property.

In addition to freestanding walls, there are retaining walls intended to create raised planting areas and terraces. Pressure from water building up behind the wall and pushing it out can be relieved by a series of drainage holes penetrating the wall, and directing water down into a gutter. Retaining walls where moisture collects and keeps the stones moist can often develop a luxurious covering of moss and a collection of ferns.

Walls need good foundations, usually a trench filled with cement or crushed stone to below the frost line, and since wall construction can be a tedious task fraught with difficulties, it is important to employ a good stonemason experienced in laying stone or brick. Local quarries not only are good places to find stonemasons; they often have display areas showing the effects possible using different kinds of stone. The type of stone used often identifies a wall with a particular part of a country – flint walls are found in the eastern counties of England, for example, and black slate is used in many Welsh walls. Smooth round river stones (called 'jacks') come from the Delaware River, in the eastern part of the USA.

In addition to choosing good facing stones – the side that people see when they pass a wall – suitable capping (or coping) stones are needed so the top sheds water. These coping stones are usually rounded, but can be flat, as in the Cotswold district of England. In Yorkshire, flat stones are up-ended to create a cap that not only sheds water but discourages people

1 Ha-ha at Rockwood garden, Delaware. 2 Blue wall with yellow grillwork, Marjorelle garden, Morocco. 3 Privacy wall, Winterthur. 4 Delaware, dry wall with rockery plants.

1 *Field stone wall crosses stream at Glen Burnie garden, Virginia.* 2 *Formal brick privacy wall with circular clairvoyee and reflecting pool, Winterhome, New Zealand.* 3 *Retaining wall, Longwood Gardens, Pennsylvania.* 4 *Centranthus on retaining wall, Bodysgallen estate, Wales.*

1

3

4

from sitting on the wall and collapsing it. Mortar – or the lack of it – is also important. Sometimes called 'pointing', the mortar can be recessed to give the appearance of a dry-wall construction, or the pointing can be set flush with the stone for a more substantial, finished look.

Other structural features can be considered with walls – the entrance, for example, can be a solid Gothic-style door if the intention is to create an historical look. Also, window slits can be used along walls to convey the impression of age, or metal grills inserted for a Mediterranean look. Walls can have niches and steps to an observation platform, catwalk or a turret. Monet trained espaliered fruit trees against high walls at the side of his house. Lean-to sheds and greenhouses can be positioned against a wall.

Walls of rough fieldstone, especially with dry-wall construction, are excellent places for plants that relish sharp drainage and tolerate dry conditions, such as wall pennywort and Kenilworth ivy. In the Vatican Gardens, Rome, there is even a high brick wall completely colonized by red valerian (*Centranthus ruber*), the roots finding moisture through the porosity of the brick. If a planted wall is desired, consider building the wall of tufa rock, a rough volcanic material with a pitted texture, riddled with air holes. Its cinder-like appear-

ance can be soon masked with plants rooting in the crevices, and tufa has the advantage of being extremely lightweight, allowing large boulders to be lifted with ease. Though the crevices in walls may be difficult to squeeze live plants into, seed of foxgloves, fleabane, lewisias, sedum, mulleins and wallflowers – pushed into cracks inside a soil plug – can be far more successful.

Where a wall discourages plant growth, for example tightly fitted brick, niches can be created to carry potted plants or sculpture, even a bench. Cement walls can be made to look less austere with a colorful or textured covering of pebbles, shells, tile or mosaic.

Be aware, however, that of the three kinds of popular barrier – wooden fences, hedges and walls – it is a wall that is usually the most costly in materials. At the same time, nothing else will provide the sense of seclusion and 'secrecy', permanence and grandeur that a stone or brick wall gives a garden.

Ha-has are walls that produce a drop-off, usually at the front or rear of a house, to prevent livestock such as sheep and cattle from wandering into ornamental plantings. Viewed from the house, the wall is hidden from view, below ground level. To make it, a ditch is dug, the side nearest the house walled, and the other side graded to create a ramp.

Waterfalls

WATERFALLS Without doubt, the best way to introduce water to a garden is through a waterfall. When one considers all the features that a garden might use to good effect, surely the sight and sound of a waterfall – sparkling alluringly and splashing musically – is the most beautiful and the most serene. Indeed, waterfalls in Oriental gardens are considered so important that garden designers have developed a lexicon of descriptions to identify them: a cascade that falls in a solid sheet is called a falling cloth; a waterfall that spills in a long, narrow stream is called a silver thread; when a dividing stone separates the falling cloth it is called a broken cloth fall; if a silver thread is split by divider stones into a series of threads the combined effect is called a multi-thread fall. Along rocky streams the placement of dividing stones can direct water to the left or right, creating stepped falls. The use of large boulders, called flanking stones, can concentrate the flow so that when it is heavy, following rainfall, it forms a falling cloth, and when it is low it forms silver threads.

Waterfalls also need base stones for foundation support, edging stones to retain the stream bank, fill stones to support the falls, observation stones for admiring the falls, and stepping stones to provide access to observation points or to cross the stream.

1

2   3

The most beautiful naturalistic waterfalls are in Japan, especially around Kyoto, where hilly terrain and nearby mountainous streams inspired garden designers to study the fluidity of water in infinite detail, bringing together water, evergreens, stone and moss in ways that even the smallest home garden today can emulate. At the other extreme, the most ostentatious examples exist in Italian Renaissance gardens, especially at the Villa d'Este where the fall of water from a clifftop creates for the visitor an astonishing vertical experience of constantly moving water.

To estimate the volume of water needed to recreate a natural waterfall, or a small formal one admired in another garden, place a gallon bucket under the flow and time how long it takes to fill the bucket. As an example, if it takes 15 seconds to fill, then the flow is four gallons per minute and a local aquatic center will be able to recommend a re-circulating pump of the appropriate size. For large or complicated falls, it is best to hire a professional to do the calculation and installation.

1 *Fountain of the Ovato, Villa d'Este, Italy.* 2 *Broken falls in a Japanese garden.* 3 *Falling cloth waterfall, Ayrlies garden, New Zealand.* 4 *Frozen falls, Frank Lloyd Wright's Fallingwater, Pennsylvania.*

4

Water gardens

WATER GARDENS Water is the essence of all life, and without it plants cannot survive. Whether it comes from the sky in the form of rain, mist or snow, or emerges from hidden ground reserves, water is such a precious commodity the sight of it is usually uplifting and beautiful. Both the ancient Chinese garden designers, seeking to create a sanctuary for scholarly meditation, and the early Persians, seeking expressions of power and prestige, made water the central focus of their gardens. The Chinese created naturalistic carp ponds fed by rocky streams exaggerated to represent fantastical rock formations. The Persians revered it within a geometry of reflecting pools, channels, runnels, rills, and glittering movement in the form of cascades, fountains, eddies and arching jets.

In modern times, the installation of artificial water features can be labor-saving or labor-intensive, depending on whether fish, pumps and filters are involved. Fortunate is the garden that already has a natural water feature, such as a wildlife pond, splashing cascade or murmuring stream, for these generally require minimal embellishment and maintenance. Water is the music of nature and still water has the ability to double the beauty of its surroundings through reflections. Few know how to play the musical keyboard with water better than the Japanese. They tumble it in a series of waterfalls and rock pools, regulating the flow and fall to produce splashes, gurgles and slaps against rocks. They ripple it over shallow streams where it gleams and glitters in the sunlight.

Still water is a mirror, reflecting poolside plantings, arched bridges, gazebos and other appropriate garden accents. On cloudy days when the surface turns opaque, water produces a mysterious quality. Even in the space of a small garden the

1

3

4

5

6

7

2

1 *Monet's water garden.*
2 *Formal waterlily pool, Kansas.* 3
*Tropical pool, Marjorelle garden,
Morocco.* 4 *Kidney-shaped pool.*
5 *Rainbow, Swiss Pines Japanese garden,
Pennsylvania.* 6 *Circular pool, Blake
House, California.* 7 *Cloud-shaped pool,
Ladew Topiary Gardens, Maryland.*
8 *Pool designed by Ohme and Van
Sweden for suburban Maryland home.*

8

3

4

1

5

2

presence of water can be used in a variety of ways, perhaps none better than a reflecting pool filled with the flashing images of fish.

Water gardens can be classified as formal and informal. Formal shapes include circular, oval, rectangular and square. Informal gardens tend to be kidney-shaped or cloud-shaped. The geometric shapes of formal pools can echo the architectural lines of an adjacent structure, such as a residence, and so they are popular in courtyards. Formal pools can also introduce a surprise element to a naturalistic setting, such as woodland.

The lining of a pool must be waterproof, and generally there are four choices – a clay liner that is impervious to water, a concrete liner, a rigid pre-formed liner and a flexible liner. Clay liners can work well unless there are musk rats, turtles or water snakes that can burrow through the clay and cause leakage. Concrete is labor-intensive and prone to cracking. Rigid liners are good for small pools, and flexible liners are good for large ones. Try to dispense with as many pond accessories as possible, including filters and pumps that can clog, rust, leak,

6

short out, or break down. A clear pool is possible by using natural water filters such as oxygenating plants and fish.

With rigid or flexible liners, installation is relatively easy. Small pools or ponds can be excavated by hand. Beneath the liner base and up the sides should be filled with a two-inch layer of sand to prevent damage to the liner. The liner's top can be hidden with a rim of flat, heavy stones, and the surrounding area planted with iris and ornamental grasses to further blur the edges.

Waterlilies are best grown in submerged pots. When choosing waterlilies, there are hardy and tropical kinds. The hardies float their star-shaped flowers on the water surface, and they come mostly in pink, red, yellow, orange and white. The tropicals are tender and larger flowered. Also, they will provide an extra four weeks of bloom compared to the hardies. The tropicals hold their heads above the water on long flower stalks, and the color range is more extensive, including blue and purple. The hardies will survive winter providing they remain in water below the freeze line. The tropicals must be taken indoors and stored in tanks that never ice over.

1 *Small pool with bridge and fountain.* 2 *Moss-covered, natural falls, Glen Burnie Chinese garden, Virginia.* 3 *Stepped cascade, Cross Hills Garden, New Zealand.* 4 *Formal rill and pool with Amazon waterlily platters, Wertz Farm, Pennsylvania.* 5 *Small-scale Japanese-style pool, Rotorua, New Zealand.* 6 *Formal water garden, Winterhome, New Zealand.*

Wellheads

WELLHEADS can be purely functional, providing irrigation for gardens that must rely on underground water reserves, or they can be a decorative accent for herb or vegetable gardens and courtyards. Moreover, a wellhead can identify a theme. For example, there are Japanese-style wellheads, with a system of wooden pulleys, sisal ropes and wooden buckets. European well-heads, from Provence and Tuscany in particular, can feature carved stone and marble, often with ornate wrought-iron decoration, metal buckets and supports for the pulley chains. Well shafts are usually raised to waist height for the transfer of water and the raised section is generally circular or multi-sided, such as hexagonal.

Many styles of American wellheads can be seen today at Colonial Williamsburg, Virginia, most of them within a well-house – a wooden-roofed enclosure – where the well shaft itself is covered with a hinged lid to ensure safety and prevent unwanted animals or leaf litter falling down to contaminate the water.

In the 19th century, hand-cranked metal pumps began to replace traditional stone wells and their system of wooden superstructure and pulleys. These metal pumps can feature as decorative accents, particularly in herb gardens.

1 Thatched wellhead, Keukenhof, Holland. 2 Tuscan wellhead, Mill House Garden, Connecticut. 3 Tuscan wellhead, Cranbrook house, Michigan. 4 Hand pump, Blades Farm, Yorkshire.

1

2

3

4

Wheels

WHEELS have many practical but also purely decorative uses in the garden. Functionally, they can take the form of a waterwheel along a stream, where a flow of water diverted along a sluice will turn the wheel and even generate power. Wheels are also prominent features of decorative small carts and wheelbarrows, especially chunky wooden types that can be a focal point in a vegetable, herb or cutting garden.

Rusty metal wheels are useful to make all kinds of garden ornamentation – for example, a moveable bench. Welded together, such wheels can also make a funky fence or the rails for a bridge. Small wheels will serve as edging, part of each one embedded in soil to make a scalloped design.

At Cedaridge Farm a large metal tractor wheel has been laid flat on the ground close to the kitchen to create a miniature culinary herb garden, with parsley, sage, chives, basil and thyme growing between the spokes. At Rathmoy, an estate garden in New Zealand's North Island, wheels from an assortment of farm implements are suspended above eye level to support top-knots of climbing roses, their canes spreading out when they reach the wheel, and cascading down to make a curtain of flowers.

Perhaps the most desirable wheel to consider in garden design is the millstone, which can be used alone to make a decorative accent leaning against a stone wall, or several can be laid flat on the ground to make beautiful stepping stones.

1 *Millstone, Winterthur, Delaware.* 2 *Metal water wheel, Chanticleer garden, Pennsylvania.* 3 *Wagon wheel bridge rails, New Zealand.* 4 *Cart used as a planter, Casa Pacifica, California.* 5 *Wagon wheel bench, Clatterburn garden, New Zealand.*

1

3

5

4

Whimsy

WHIMSY in the garden can take many forms: an amusing anecdote engraved on stone, a funny scarecrow in a vegetable garden, an animated topiary figure, such as Mickey Mouse or Goofy. Whimsy is a way of reflecting a garden owner's personality. For example, Harvey S. Ladew, founder of the Ladew Topiary Gardens, near Baltimore, loved foxhunting, so one of his more amusing topiary pieces shows a fox chased by four hounds and rider, shaped out of Japanese yew (see page 189). In a summerhouse that used to be the ticket office for the Savoy Theater in London, Ladew had a secret bar hidden behind a mirror for entertaining visitors, and a couch with a cushion that read 'Love thy neighbor, but do it discreetly.' In another area, called the Orchard Garden, where he underplanted a collection of apple trees with azaleas, he placed a pair of statues representing Eve tempting Adam with an apple. Elsewhere a pleached statue of Buddha ensures the gardens are interdenominational.

Garden gnomes are whimsical ornaments, and though many folks would not be caught dead with one in their garden, Albert duPont, founder of Nemours Garden, Delaware, an imitation of Versailles Palace, France, created a village of gnomes, mushrooms and witches. Located along a stream, below an arched stone bridge, its purpose is to raise eyebrows or produce a laugh or two.

With tongue in cheek, Felder Rushing, in a popular book about gardening in Southern USA, declared that the only improvement for two plastic pink flamingoes on a lawn was to have a hundred. But perhaps the most whimsical garden of all is the coastal property of New Zealand artist Lindsay Crooks, who creates colorful three-dimensional animated figures for decorating the outdoors, offering them for sale and giving them appropriate names like 'The Weeder', 'The Planter', and 'The Sunbather'.

1 *Lindsay Crooks sculpture, New Zealand.* 2 *Flower pot scarecrows, Rathmoy, New Zealand.* 3 *Topiary Buddha.* 4 *Whimsical scarecrow, potager garden, France.* 5 *Pair of pink flamingoes.*

3

5

4

Wildflowers

WILDFLOWERS 'The preservation of the earth is in wildness,' wrote the American conservationist, Henry Thoreau. Though cultivated flower gardens are good to have around the house, wildflower plantings can make a beautiful transition between garden and wilderness. Establishing a colony of wildflowers is possible by purchasing a widely adapted wildflower seed mixture and sowing it onto bare soil in a sunny position in spring and autumn. Unless bare soil is provided, seed germination may be hindered by more aggressive weeds and native grasses.

Ready-made wildflower mixtures can be purchased for specific needs: for example, a woodland mix, meadow mix, annuals mix, perennials and annuals mix, tall mix, short mix, butterfly mix, and mixtures that produce seed for songbirds. There are also mixtures of wildflowers specific to a particular area.

Most commercial 'wildflower' mixtures do not contain native plant species. They are formulated from introduced flowering annuals that will naturalize readily in a wide range of soils. Popular components of inexpensive wildflower mixtures include California poppies, African daisies, Texas bluebonnets, European corn poppies and Mediterranean mallows, a fast-growing collection which would never be seen mingling in their natural state, but thrives in most sunny, garden soils, and therefore collectively, gives the impression of a natural wildflower colony.

The most challenging of all wildflower projects is to create a special habitat for the preservation of an endangered wildflower species: for example, pink lady's slipper orchids in woodland, or pitcher plants or cobra lilies in a boggy area. Seek advice from specialist growers on the Internet, or a specialist wildflower sanctuary, for help with this type of conservation effort.

3

1 *Colony of cobra lilies, Oregon.*
2 *Evening primrose meadow,*
Texas. 3 *Benner woodland garden,*
Pennsylvania. 4 *Bluebonnets and*
Indian paintbrush, Houston, Texas.

4

The biggest problem with establishing a wildflower colony is competition from aggressive weeds and grasses. These can quickly crowd out seeded wildflower mixtures, making the result look sparse. One way around this is to plough the area every spring so the wildflowers at least have a chance of becoming established, or seed in late summer and autumn of the previous flowering season when activity from weeds slows down. The wildflower seed will germinate during cool weather and at the onset of cold winter weather, the top growth will go dormant. Growth will renew at the onset of warm spring temperatures, causing the green crowns to produce flower stems extra early in the season.

The two most common types of wildflower habitat are meadow (or prairie) and woodland, though there are also alpine, desert and bog, among others.

1 *Wildflower planting with poppies, Cedaridge Farm.*
2 *Strawflower meadow.* 3 *Cottage garden wildflower mixture.*
4 *African daisies, Clanwilliam Wildflower Preserve, South Africa.*

Window boxes

WINDOW BOXES allow plants to be grown beneath windowsills. The long, narrow, deep rectangular wooden construction of traditional designs allows for a parade of plants, either all one variety (such as ivy-leaf geraniums), or mixed kinds. Where the squarish shape of a window box looks rather severe, metal hayrack planters make good alternatives. These are shaped like a cradle, to fit flat against a wall, with an iron grillwork and a liner of coconut matting or sphagnum moss to hold in the soil. Plants can be planted below the rim, through the matting, to gain a much fuller effect than traditional window-box planters.

Spring bulbs and primulas make good subjects early in the season. Later, spreading and cascading plants are ideal for summer displays, including annual alyssum, lobelia, nasturtiums, petunia and verbena since these are 'everblooming.' Good foliage plants to mix with them are velvety plectranthus, silvery licorice plant (*Helichrysum*) and fountain grass.

Where a wall does not feature a window, window-box planters can be affixed below a faux window, such as a mirror or a section of trellis shaped like a window.

Window boxes are prone to drying out quickly and so moisture retentive soil is advisable. Though mixtures of commercial potting soil and garden topsoil are better than potting soil alone, the addition of water-retaining crystals will help keep up moisture levels, yet allow excess water to drain away.

Window boxes must be securely fastened, for growing plants, when soaked with rain, can become exceedingly heavy and tear a weak holder from the wall.

1 *Cottage window box, Cedaridge Farm.*
2 *Daffodils, Keukenhof, Holland.* 3 *Cascading lobelia.*
4 *Ivy-leaf geraniums, Switzerland.*

1

2

4

3

Windows

W

WINDOWS are essential for viewing gardens from the house, and many landscape architects will begin a design project by looking out at the property from a house's interior. Windows can also provide a porthole in a garden wall or fence, and they can embellish the wall of a building to provide an ethnic identity: for example, a Moorish window with ornate grillwork, or a Chinese window with distinctive cobalt-blue willow-pattern tiles. At Cedaridge Farm there is even a faux window made from a mirror, its principal purpose to make the blank wall more decorative and to provide an excuse for a window box. Plantings of foxgloves and other tall flowers are deliberately made opposite the faux window so an exquisite reflection is seen.

Sir Edwin Lutyens, the Victorian architect who collaborated with Gertrude Jekyll on many projects, designed a special tall, narrow window for the stairway of houses he planned. Not only do such windows provide a strong, vertical accent when viewed from the garden (the house at Parc Floral des Moutiers, France, illustrates this well) but they also allow a home's occupants a spectacular outside view when they descend the main interior staircase.

Windows in most situations are for looking out at a beautiful view. 'Clairvoyees' are windows cut into a boundary or interior garden wall to allow a view of the countryside beyond. These are usually circular or arched and can be set with a metal grill for security. If a scenic view does not exist, perhaps a vista can be cut through woodland to create an extended view to a gazebo on the horizon, or the garden space immediately beyond the window planted to provide a tapestry of color.

1

2

3

1 *Sir Edwin Lutyens residence, near Dieppe.*
2 *Clairvoyee, Colonial Williamsburg.* **3** *Chinese-style window.*
4 *Chinese-style clairvoyee and grillwork.* **5** *View from studio, Madoo garden, New York State.*

5

4

Woodland gardens

1 *Ruth Levitan's woodland garden, Connecticut.*
2 *Winterthur garden, Delaware.* 3 *Bluebell woods and azaleas.*
4 *Daffodil display, Magnolia Plantation, South Carolina.*

WOODLAND GARDENS can be exceedingly beautiful, and provide many levels of interest, from the ground to the overhead tree canopy. The trunks of trees can present strong upright structural elements, contrasts of sunlight and shadow can produce an ever-changing scene, and of course a woodland garden can be a cool place to seek refuge on a hot day. However, there are many kinds of woodland, each type with its own ecosystem, some conducive to growing flowering plants, others that will inhibit plant growth. Some trees produce a toxin from their roots which is detrimental to most other plants. Dense shade or compacted soil from tree roots also forms a barrier close to the soil's surface which sometimes prevents plant growth.

Deciduous woodland generally is easier to cultivate than evergreen woodland because deciduous trees lose their leaves in winter, allowing certain flowering plant species to break through the soil at the first sign of a warming trend in spring. Many woodland wildflowers will set seed and begin dispersing their seeds even before the trees are in full leaf. Spring flowers such as hellebore, aconites, snowdrops, woodland phlox and trillium fit into this category.

Evergreens tend to maintain such dense shade all year

1

3

4

2

round that it is much more difficult to find flowering plants to thrive under them, without rigorously thinning the canopy. In evergreen woodland, rather than try to cultivate flowering plants, it may be better to thin the lower branches and keep the woodland floor clean for the establishment of a shady monoculture such as moss growth or ferns, both of which will tolerate deep shade. Rather than paths made from hardscape material, such as flagstone, woodland paths defined by pine needles, wood chips or shredded leaves will look more natural.

Where woodland soil is compacted or tree roots form a barrier to planting, consider carting in good topsoil and creating raised beds around trees, using thick branches or rough stone to mound up the soil. Do not mound soil against the trunk, however, since this can cause rot.

When looking to establish a woodland garden, consider at least four layers of interest – the ground floor, which can be planted with groundcover plants such as cyclamen and bluebells; the herbaceous level, using shade-loving plants like hostas and ferns; the shrub level (from eye level to understorey height) using shrubby plants or small trees like rhododendrons and redbuds; and the canopy, using tall trees like maples and oaks that can arch out their branches and knit together to form a high green cover of foliage. These layers are not finite, since the tendency for plants to grow at different rates will result in interlacing and a blurring of the layers. Aesthetically, layering produces a strong impact on the eye since it fills one's entire view with interest.

1 Asiatic lilies, Deerfield, Pennsylvania.
2 Autumn-blooming cyclamen beneath Austrian pine.
3 Woodland walk, Cedaridge Farm. 4 Rhododendron and bog primulas, Lady Horlicks garden, Scotland.

Conclusion: The garden as art

Bridge, lake and temple, Stourhead, England.

In the early years of civilization, humans sought to control nature, to tame the fearsome wilderness, to mold it to a satisfying orderliness, and imbue it with comforting psychological meaning. The desire to create garden spaces as symbols of power and prestige among potentates became entwined with religious beliefs to such an extent that in Imperial China, the talents of philosopher, scholar and painter were often qualifications needed to be hired as a garden-maker.

In his masterful book, *The English Garden* (Thames & Hudson, 1964), Edward Hyams declared that the evolution of the contemporary English garden is the story of a search for paradise. I would contend it is not the only reason. Surely the images in this book point to a more deep-seated reason why people today create gardens – a desire to express a sense of artistry.

Paradise can be found in the misty mountain glens of Scotland, the deserts of Africa, the rainforests of Brazil, the river valleys of northeastern United States, the deserted sandy beaches of Australia and New Zealand. Though a paradise may be the end result of the most successful garden design, surely it is the expression of artistry that is the main catalyst today to mold our surroundings into something visually more uplifting.

Even Hyams praised banker Henry Hoare's Stourhead, in England, as the world's most beautiful landscape setting, stating, 'Now it is a fact that Stourhead as Hoare made it was one of the masterpieces of European art, and for many who realized this the introduction of flowering shrubs into the picture was an outrage. For horticultural aesthetists, it was as if the owner of a Rembrandt who disliked the darkness of the picture, took a palette of bright colors and a brush and proceeded to brighten it up a bit.'

Claude Monet's garden at Giverny is undeniably a paradise, but the artist already considered Giverny to be a painter's paradise when he first saw it fleetingly from the window of a train. He described the garden he created at Giverny as his greatest work of art, revealing that it was his artistic yearnings that were the impetus for his garden.

Perhaps it is the ephemeral quality of gardens that often causes observers to overlook them as works of art. Put a picture in the attic, and its value will only increase over time, but ignore a garden for more than a week, and it will start to revert to wilderness.

My own garden, Cedaridge Farm, was a paradise of lawns, meadows, woodland and mature trees even before I planted a single daffodil, and when I started to design its garden spaces, every structure and every plant was placed with infinite care, not so much to enhance something that was already beautiful, but to impose my own sense of artistry on the natural landscape, using both plants and structures to paint a pretty picture.

About the author

Born and educated in England, Derek Fell is a widely published garden writer and garden photographer, now living in the United States. The author of more than 100 garden books and garden calendars, he has won more awards from the Garden Writers Association of America than any other person. A consultant to the White House on garden design during the Ford Administration, Fell's award-winning books include *Great Gardens of New Zealand* (Bateman), *Van Gogh's Gardens* (Simon & Schuster), *550 Home Landscaping Ideas* (Simon & Schuster), *Deerfield Garden – An American Garden through Four Seasons* (Pidcock Press), *Secrets of Monet's Garden* (Metro Books) and *A Photographer's Garden* (Kodak).

His articles about gardens and garden design have appeared in publications worldwide, including *Architectural Digest* (USA), *The Garden* (the magazine of the Royal Horticultural Society, Great Britain), and *The New Zealand Gardener*.

Married, with three children, Fell cultivates an award-winning garden at historic Cedaridge Farm, Pennsylvania.

For more information visit his website www.derekfell.net

The author photographing Asiatic lilies, Cedaridge Farm.

Acknowledgements

There are many people I need to thank for helping me amass this immense volume of images showing so many aspects of garden design, starting in 1959 when I was inspired by my friend, the late Harry Smith, British garden photographer, to purchase a camera and start shooting gardens worldwide. My wife, Carolyn, a landscape designer, has accompanied me to many gardens, and with her discerning eye often pointed out unusual garden features I might have overlooked.

The Departments of Tourism for Great Britain, France, New Zealand, Morocco, South Africa, Brazil, Australia and Holland all helped me with introductions to beautiful gardens, and also with travel arrangements.

Some of the designers whose work is featured in this book include Carter van Dyke, Marshall Brickman, Hiroshi Makita, Robyn Kilty, Rosa Stepanova, Charles Gale, Jack Miller, Renny Reynolds, Timothy and Isabelle Vaughan, Trish Bartleet, Wolfgang Oehme, James Van Sweden, Sir Miles Warren, Lucy Dorrien-Smith, Kurt Blumell, Princess Greta Sturdza, Andy Goldsworthy, Lindsay Crooks, and the Plimpton design team.

Thanks also to my office manger, Joan Haas, for maintaining my collection of 150,000 horticultural images, and the many garden owners worldwide who invited me to photograph their beautiful gardens.

The author's Cedaridge Farm serves as an outdoor studio for artistic photography.

Index

Bold face indicates reference in a photo caption and capitalized names indicate main design categories, with the asterisks denoting the featured pages.